# HYPHENED-NATION

*don't check the box*

by

NICOLE DRAFFEN

# ACKNOWLEDGEMENTS

There are many people to thank for making this book a reality. I especially want to thank my niece Skyler. She inspired me to write this book. I needed to make certain she grew up with an enlightened viewpoint of who she is as an American, and specifically an American of color.

My editor Joel for guiding me so tirelessly through the editing process. Your direction and provocative insight guided me along this journey, and made me go down paths of thought, I may have hesitated to venture.

In a much broader sense, I'd like to thank my close friends in the United Kingdom. Each of you in your own special way taught me how to be my own authentic self.

Thank you to my family who patiently listened to and provided insight on endless edits. It's been a journey.

Ironically, with the concluding of the book, it sparks a new beginning...

# INTRODUCTION

*"I am not concerned that you have fallen --*
*I am concerned that you arise."*

—Abraham Lincoln;

I might as well get it out of the way. Some of you may feel I'm not qualified to write this book. I don't hold any degrees from our country's prestigious universities. I enjoy reading about history, but I am no scholar. I am neither a sophisticated globetrotter nor an expert on foreign affairs.

I am, however, someone who loves to learn about other cultures. This book tells my story of how living amid another culture in another country opened my eyes to my place in my own country. It was a three-week visit in 2009 to run a marathon in Wales and see the sights in London that turned into a year-long immersion.

But it also resulted in a personal discovery: seeing my own identity in my own country. In short, I felt like a true American for the first time in my life.

Now, I should mention that I love America and feel I am a true patriot. Not in the "my country right or wrong" sense or with a blind spot to how so much of America was built on the oppression of people of color. No, I am a patriot because I believe I have a duty to my country, myself and my fellow Americans to ensure our leaders live up to the inspiring ideas in the words of our Constitution—especially when those words are used to subvert what I feel to be their underlying truth.

But while I loved America, and thought I knew what it was, my extended stay away helped me to better understand certain aspects. Check that: I realized there were some aspects of my country that I *didn't* understand, particularly how Americans view themselves as Americans.

My stay in the U.K. was the first time I felt truly classified as an American. I was born and raised in California, but I am classified as an African American simply because my skin is brown and some of my ancestors hailed from the African continent. In reality, I am a mix of African, French, Scottish and Native American blood. Yet because of the hue of my skin, I am immediately termed one thing—and that isn't even a "full" American, but one with the word African in front of it.

I thought the reason for terms that put individuals into groups was to break down a large body of people into smaller units to more efficiently and communicate with them, such as in presidential campaigns. Considering the vast diversity of America—not just the ethnic and cultural diversity we hear so much about in this era of identity politics, but also age, socio-economic, geography, all the different factors that shape our perspectives--it would be logistically impossible for any candidate to reach them all with one message. So instead of a unifying message to all Americans, we get ones tailored specifically to smaller groups of Americans: seniors or millennials; suburban soccer moms or rural residents; LGBTQ or so-called straight Americans.

But nowhere are Americans viewed less as one collective, unified people with a shared concern and vision and more as smaller groups with competing--if not opposing—concerns, than in terms of race and ethnicity. And regardless if those terms have, or had, hyphens (African-American, Arab-American, Mexican-American) or don't (black Hispanic, Latino), it is my contention in this book that the words and ways others use to describe *what* we are —and which we often call ourselves—do a disservice to *who* we truly are.

Those words, which may have once been used with pride, have turned into labels, which now sow disunity, distrust and even a palpable sense in 2020 America that there are only two kinds of Americans:

1) Real Americans who need no other descriptor or qualifier than the color of their skin.

2) Every other American, who needs something qualifying them as such.

It will take work to change the perception that skin color defines a genuine American; because, as I will relate in this book, that perception existed before America did. And even though that perception is not shared by all Americans, it remains strong.

As an example, as I was finishing some rewrites on the second edition of this book, which I originally wrote in 2015, one of the many mini-eruptions sparked by U.S. President Donald Trump consumed the airwaves: his July 2019 comment that four outspoken female members of Congress, all of whom are ethnic minorities, should "go back to where they're from," if they have problems with America.

The president saying that didn't surprise me; though I don't intend this to be a political book in terms of pro-Trump or anti-Trump, anyone paying attention knows that he says and Tweets things that are startling to say the least. But while the reaction of those upset about that quote (three of the Congresswomen were born in America, one is naturalized) was expected, I didn't anticipate his remarks would be so applauded by his base, such as the crowd at a Trump rally the next day that chanted "Send Her Back" for nearly 10 seconds after the president mentioned one of the four women during his speech.

But I should have. One thing I have learned in the process of researching and writing this book that in terms of what makes a person a "real American," the color of a person's skin is more important than whether they were born here or how long they have lived here.

I have lived here my entire life, but I never truly felt more like a real American than when I was treated as one outside of America. That inspired me to write this book, for finally feeling that way made me feel so proud. But it also made me determined to abolish the hyphen, and any other racial and ethnic descriptors designed to divide rather than unite.

More than a century of using the hyphen and other convenient identifiers of ethnicity and race has resulted in the marginalization and reduction of all but one group of Americans. These labels haven't given members of ethnic groups a sense of collective identity, or made them feel like active, important, contributing parts of a greater whole; they have rendered them somehow not fully American.

And that must stop.

I hope you will not only enjoy reading this book, but that it will make you realize, reflect upon and, most importantly, act to change, the reality that even the subtlest overtones of discrimination can affect human experience and relationships across generations.

# CHAPTER ONE

---

# THE MANTLE

*"You are growing into consciousness, and my wish for you is that you feel no need to constrict yourself to make other people comfortable."*

—Ta-Nehisi Coates

I 'd like to introduce you to a concept I call the "Mantle of Consciousness." It is something I believe every so-called minority in America lives with, but few truly recognize. It is a protective cloak that develops around you without you even realizing it, a layer of psychic insulation that shields you from a disquieting feeling that you are somehow different from so much that surrounds you: the people on TV and in the movies; the faces on billboards and other advertisements. If it were not for the mantle buffering you from those feelings, a person's sense of self could easily short-circuit, rendering them isolated and separate, a constant reminder that they don't truly belong.

That mantle drapes around you like a well-worn cotton shirt that, after many washings, feels paper-thin, yet still clings to you like a shadow.

It took a trip to another country to understand that my mantle was not there to protect me from the feeling that the color of my skin made me inferior to others; but that how I was labeled because of that skin color made me feel less than a real American.

The mantle changes as one matures. As a child, it is light and ephemeral because children live in the moment. We jump in puddles, blissfully unaware that other people are getting splashed. We smile and talk to everyone, wholeheartedly enjoying ourselves and never contemplating that others may be scrutinizing us as something different than what we know we are: ourselves. In itself, that is a beautiful thing; it allows minority children to enjoy their lives without the encumbrance of societal labels. But the carefree bliss of early years is eventually replaced by a new knowledge of inequality, and the mantle grows heavier.

By the time I entered junior high, my mantle was weighing on me. I had already noticed the cartoons I loved on Saturday mornings, mostly the "Looney Tunes" cast of Bugs Bunny, Daffy Duck and Porky Pig, usually portrayed any brown character as an illiterate imbecile.

Or they were streetwise hustlers, talking in jive, otherwise known as "Negro slang," such as the black crows in Disney's "Dumbo" as well as King Louis in "The Jungle Book." Even at that age, it wasn't hard to pick up on the less-than-subtle message that brown and black either meant dumb or token, superficial characters meant to be ridiculed.

Associating darker colors with negativity was reinforced in real life whenever my mother took me shopping. I noticed most of the dolls in department stores looked like miniature white little girls, but the few black ones had skin the color of coal, or enlarged red lips and other facial features, or unkempt hair. I knew plenty of black kids—none of them looked like that!

And then there were the books. I devoured any book I could get my hands on. But I began noticing those with prominent black characters, like "The Adventures of Huckleberry Finn," and "To Kill a Mockingbird" were always speaking in patois English, what I would later realize was American slave English, a predecessor to Ebonics.

Those characters didn't reflect my reality, neither did those cartoons or those dolls. Their reality existed somewhere else, I thought, outside of mine.

But then I began noticing the stares from people when my aunt Angel took me shopping. She was white, something that never struck me as unusual, but whenever

I called her aunt Angel in public, strangers snapped their heads around and looked at me with puzzled faces. It slowly dawned on me that for many people, a black girl calling a white woman aunt wasn't the way things were supposed to be. I began feeling that I stood out to those people as much as the crude dolls and grotesque cartoon caricatures of people of color stood out to me.

And then it hit me: I was the odd one. I didn't fit in. But rather than proud of being different from the majority, I felt at times embarrassed or even ashamed, like I didn't belong, didn't deserve the same opportunities as others. That is when I first felt what I would eventually realize was cultural inequality; that while I might be learning in history class that America was built on the concepts of equality and liberty, I lived in a different America. A country where inequality was the norm and the perceptions of others were more important than what I thought of myself.

I think I first felt the seriousness of this in sixth grade. After cast as the lead in a play, I rushed home flushed with excitement and immediately began attempting to learn my lines by reciting them out loud. The next day, I was in the principal's office with my mom, who happened to be president of the PTA. She had heard me working on my lines and was horrified: my character was a prostitute, as were all the black characters. My mother said not only would I not be in the play, but it had better not be produced at all.

I was more upset that I wouldn't be in the play, but my mom saw the real problem: the first exposure her little girl had to the world of theater was a play in which she played a black prostitute. I long since forgot the name of the play, but today I realize this was my first exposure to the low expectations that society had for me, expectations that I believe were heavily influenced by media portrayals of race on TV. I was barely 12 years old. But I had become aware of something no child should ever have to deal with.

I can only imagine what other young children of color experience. Because trust me, if a middle-class black child living in a decent neighborhood could pick up on cues from strangers and the media that there was something about them that was different, less than equal, anyone could.

I spent my formative years in a stable two-parent household. My dad worked at a Fortune 500 company; my mother studied gerontology and directed a retirement facility. Both were educated and spoke English articulately. Even when my parents separated when I was 10, the household dynamic did not significantly change.

But even though I felt safe, protected and loved, as I grew into adolescence and evolved from watching cartoons and into watching regular TV sitcoms and dramas, the images took on a far more unsettling tone.

The black or brown people I saw on TV always seemed poor and struggling to get from day to day. Even the good things that happened seemed like meager crumbs that had fallen from a table they weren't allowed to sit at. It was as if the best life could offer people of color was to be content with small victories, like making rent at the last second or getting out of a parking ticket.

Shows like "Good Times," What's Happening," and "Sanford and Son" all featured black characters struggling in inner cities, and most of them spoke in very poor English. They were hustlers, break-dancers, GARBAGE MEN. Even those shows in which the black folks "made it," they were viewed as aberrations, like George Jefferson, whose "making it" meant he could live in a skyscraper along "normal" white people, and the two brothers in "Different Strokes," who made it thanks to a wealthy white man.

I sat and watched, baffled by how the characters and settings on those programs were so different from "Happy Days," "The Partridge Family," and the "Brady Bunch." Here were families not mired in poverty, who spoke well, living in what seemed a different world than black families, one in which every episode ended with a happy message of hope and belonging.

It seemed that to be black on the TV meant your happy ending was scraping up enough money to avoid eviction, or narrowly evading the police busting you over some hustle. At what point does that lead any child to believe that happy endings are only for white people? When does a child of color, who sees no positive role models on the screen, start thinking there is a reason why people who look like them don't deserve the same chance at happiness? When do they even start wishing they hadn't been born with the skin on their bodies?

I never did, since I had plenty of positive role models. But as I started picking up on these messages, I began to understand the reality of how I was perceived by others. And my mantle grew heavier. Each new insight created another thin layer that pressed on my psyche and wove itself into the fabric of my identity.

But thanks to my supportive and educated parents, I fashioned my mantle into a flexible and protective garment that afforded me awareness, humor, and resilience. If I had not been raised in such an environment, my mantle might have become a straitjacket, restricting clear thought. My perception and judgment could have been distorted. Every encounter that had something to do with the color of my skin—especially if it reinforced the notion that I was different from the dominant white society and thus not equal—would have sparked either hostility or resignation rather than with the intelligence and humor I developed.

I still wear that mantle. Even though I am older, wiser, more experienced, it's still there. The odd thing is that I forget it exists at times, especially when socializing or working with a group of people with whom I feel comfortable. Then suddenly, I find myself in a situation where I am being observed, critiqued, or judged, based on stereotypical racial imagery. Then my mantle softly wraps itself around me like a protective force field to deflect the ignorance I encounter. But my mantle isn't just passive and reactive, nor does anyone else's have to be. Yes, it acts like a shield protecting us mentally, emotionally and spiritually. But we can also learn how to use it to cope when encountering intolerance or ignorance.

For instance, my mantle has played a significant factor in my ability to debate and to remain unemotional in emotionally charged situations, and even to use humor to my advantage.

As an example, in the early 1990s, I worked as a meter reader for the company that still employs me. I was working a route in Lake Forest, an affluent South Orange County bedroom community. I noticed a man walking a beautiful bloodhound. I love dogs, so I knelt to pet it and complimented the man on the dog's coat. Obviously proud of his dog, he commenced to give me the animal's history and pedigree. At one point, he boasted:

"Yes, this dog is from a long line of dogs that used to hunt runaway sla- "

He came to a stammering halt and just stared at me, shock and shame etched onto his face as he realized how close he had come to saying *that* word. In an instant, I felt my entire body grow hot and stiff with embarrassment, both for him and for myself. My face felt like a mask as I struggled to maintain my happy exterior while my mind raced with a million questions. *Does he look at me and think 'slave'? Why would he name that as something to be proud of?*

This internal struggle lasted only mere seconds, but it seemed much longer before I could I calmly smile and finish his word.

"Slaves?" I replied. "That's a pretty interesting pedigree."

As I so often did, I played it off with humor. But inside, I was startled at the depth of my disappointment over his words, because even though slavery is a shameful part of America's history, I have never considered it a taboo subject. Apparently, it wasn't taboo to him either – *unless* he was conversing with someone who appeared to be of African descent. *That* I do find to be shameful.

Yet, I must admit the memory now makes me laugh because of the priceless look on his face. Even though I was still aware of my mantle, I thank God that my parents gave me a healthy sense of self, which allowed me to laugh it off (even though it still stung) and left us both with some semblance of dignity.

In that situation, my mantle protected me from feeling wounded by ridiculous off-handed comments. But rather than view it solely as a passive protective cloak, I see it also as a coat of armor, one that like Tony Stark's Iron Man suit can be weaponized, albeit in a less direct manner. It allows me the space to use my sense of humor, or to take a step back from the moment and realize that comments such as I've relayed say far more about the speaker than the unintended target, myself.

My point in relating the concept of the mantle is to illustrate that being born a minority in America is not easy. It necessitates being constantly vigilant against allowing the slights, stings and arrows to pierce one's skin too deeply. For to enable them to penetrate our mantle risks becoming distracted from the one goal that I believe every American who has ever had to don the mantle should strive for: to change the system that tolerates, promotes and even benefits from labeling people, and making them feel less authentically American as others.

But these realizations about my mantle did not come easily. I easily could have spent my life wrapped in a cocoon of ignorance, oblivious that my mantle existed primarily because I was not entirely accepted as a person in my own country.

And it took leaving that country to fully understand what my mantle represented and to realize that America was not the diverse, tolerant nation I'd longed to believe in, but was built on a foundation of racial exclusion that continues today. An America in which ethnicity, not actual citizenship, is used to determine how "real" of an American you are. A non-United States of America in which racial separatism is intrinsically based on an ethnic perception vastly perpetuated by the American media.

# CHAPTER TWO

---

# AN EPIPHANY

*Difference is of the essence of humanity. Difference*
*is an accident of birth and it should therefore never be the*
*source of hatred or conflict. The answer to difference is to*
*respect it. Therein lies a most fundamental principle of*
*peace: respect for diversity."*

—John Hume (Irish Politician,
1998 Nobel Peace Prize Winner

B y the time I stepped on English soil, my mantle
was on high alert. I knew I would be judged in
the U.K. based on the color of my skin, just like
America. But you would not be reading these words if
that is what had happened.

But first, why was I there? Well, in 2010, I had three
weeks of vacation. I knew I wanted to go someplace special.
It was a no-brainer for me that meant Great Britain.

The British culture has long fascinated me, whether its films or TV, books and magazines, or the people I've met from there. I think one reason is that while there are obvious similarities between Britain and America—language, legal system, constitutionally based government—there's such a disparity in the relative sense of time. My British friends laugh when I point at a 100-year-old building in America and call it old. There are entire neighborhoods in London, not to mention towns throughout Britain, where every house was built before 1900.

Additionally, I have long been taken by the British demeanor, which seems more matter of fact, unlike so many Americans, who seem so concerned with being politically correct. That directness always surprised me; it was both off-putting and delightful at the same time.

Also, I love to run and needed somewhere that allowed me to jog and explore it thoroughly. This meant a moderate climate, as I don't like running in the heat. Finally, since I was traveling solo, I wanted a location where English was the primary language. Taking all these factors into account, the U.K. seemed like a perfect choice.

I booked my first trip in 2009 planning to run in the Snowdonia Marathon in Wales, and then visit London. Little did I suspect that trip would turn into an eventual year-long stay; or that my desire to discover another culture would lead me to discover myself within the context of my own country.

Until this trip, I'd based most of my knowledge of the world on conversations with people I'd met from other countries. But experiencing it first-hand was entirely different. Mainly, I realized how firmly embedded my minority mantle was in my psyche. Yet the more I traveled throughout the U.K., the more I felt its weight slowly dissipating.

However, I must note that my time in the U.K. was not some heavy, intense soul quest that left me raw and vulnerable but ready to grow into a new person. Nor was I looking for that. This Stella's groove was working just fine, thank you very much.

I was on vacation. I was a tourist. And I had an incredible time. While I never found the chance to cross the Irish Sea and visit Northern Ireland, I traveled across England and Scotland and ran the marathon in Wales. Wherever I went, I met fascinating people, saw awe-inspiring architecture and landscapes, and tasted culinary delights.

Whether enjoying high tea at Harrods, visiting Liverpool's famous Mathew Street (home of the Beatles), admiring art at the National Gallery in Trafalgar Square, marveling over the Westminster Abbey, or enjoying a Guinness and black currant (a dash of sweet in a bitter beer) at a pub on the River Thames while watching life sail leisurely by, I immersed myself in the iconic tourist destinations and experiences that I most wanted.

Once my initial excitement over the major landmarks in London and other big cities settled down, I ventured into the beauty of the lush green countryside and found the towns and villages possessed their own kind of architectural grandeur in the churches, castles, and pubs, many of which had been there since the 1400s.

But I also found that what truly made Britain great wasn't the iconic buildings of London or the charming quaintness of the country; it was the people. Everyone was so friendly and helpful. And perhaps that is why, although I didn't consciously realize it at the time, my mantle slowly began lifting. Even though I was a foreigner, I felt so at ease that, without trying, I started slipping out of my head, engaging in experiences with a clean slate free of preconceived notions and expectations.

One of the first indications that I was dealing with a different cultural mindset happened shortly after I arrived in England. While looking for the shoe section in a sporting goods store, I noticed a wall advertisement featuring an interracial couple embracing. I thought, "This company must be pretty badass to take this kind of chance. They are obviously not worried about losing revenue."

For a moment, in my head, I was in a store in California and felt astounded at seeing an advertisement of an interracial couple romantically embracing (and, no, this was not a Benetton ad). I then looked around and was struck by how no one else seemed to notice it; they were just going about doing their business. To them, it was just normal.

I felt like I was standing outside myself, observing my experiencing the normalcy of the moment. Then I felt something deeper, more resonant. It was like a spiritual affirmation softly telling me, "this couple is all right. Their love is good. You can love anybody." Looking back, I have to laugh that one of the first of my mini-awakenings was not shared by a single person around me. No one else seemed to give it a second thought. All I could think was:

*Toto, we are not in Kansas anymore.*

Growing up, I read countless passages that portrayed America as a melting pot. That's not the America I see today. Because that would mean everything from skin color and ethnicity to religion and gender identification would all blend into one, nothing dominating, every ingredient complementing the other and creating a new, greater whole.

If anything, we are a buffet, all the ingredients kept separate, with some getting the choice location next to the crab legs and prime rib; and others stuck in the part of the dessert section with the quivering gelatinous fruit concoctions that seem torn from the nightmares of a 1950s Betty Crocker cookbook.

Traditional British cuisine may not win any awards (although I think it has an undeserved poor rep), but in terms of diversity, it is more advanced. Whether I was visiting a village, town, or city, I was amazed not at how accepting everyone was, but how attention was never called to that acceptance. It's something that most Americans would not instinctually pick up on—unless you're an American who has felt far too often that you aren't a real American because of your skin color, or the label used to describe it.

How that has manifested in my life all too often is that people either judge me immediately based on racial perceptions or go out of their way to make sure I know they aren't judging me. They just have to mention they have black friends or make sure to drop Aretha Franklin or John Legend's name in the conversation.

No one did that in Britain. I never felt uncomfortable because someone was judging me based on conscious or unconscious bias. Nor did I feel uncomfortable because they had to mention they knew other black people. What I witnessed was an aggressive no tolerance for non-tolerance policy on anything that hinted of racism.

When I walked into a pub alone, I was almost always invited to sit by someone who genuinely wanted a conversation, regardless of any preconceived notion of who I was based on my skin color. I never got the question, "What are you?" I was merely an American visiting their town. Sure, as we began talking longer, the subject of racial relations in America and in Great Britain came up; but they were just elements of a conversation, not the reason for one.

The same with diversity. It didn't feel like Britons viewed the merging of people of different races, religions or backgrounds as something to be championed or proud about achieving, unlike America, where often it seems that merely recognizing our diversity is worthy of a medal. In Britain, diversity just is, society has evolved to such a point that diversity isn't something to be noticed.

That was apparent in British media, particularly television. I loved the air of the unexpected. Many of the television series were racially diverse; you never had to assume when you saw a person that their partner was the same ethnicity. Instead, the roles were cast with whomever the creators felt fit the part. To my Americanized viewpoint, the message coming through was, "We have overcome racial ignorance; this is just an average couple doing normal everyday things. So relax."

Regardless of the images presented, no one looked twice. Race was a non-issue. No one colored their words or behaviors to seem more relatable with who they were conversing with.

A perfect example of the unforced British integration of diversity came during the opening ceremony of the 2012 Olympics in London. I'd been back from the

U.K. for a little over a year, and watching it unfold was proof that my views on how differently the British view ethnicity were not a delusion.

It was a scene of a white woman driving up to a brick house in a MINI Cooper. Her young biracial son got out of the car with her and she entered the house where their extended family was gathered. She greeted her family and her husband, who was black, kissed her. It was so satisfying, and I felt proud to see this multi-ethnic scene.

As I watched, it reminded me once again of a place where no one gave a second glance to an ethnically diverse couple. I hoped that millions of my fellow Americans could also share in my understanding of this cultural revelation—that noticing the diversity, celebrating our differences, wasn't nearly as important as the decision to stop giving a damn about them!

Now, with that being said, I'm not putting England on some pedestal regarding all race relations. An unfortunate reminder that old habits are hard to kick was the British tabloid press treatment of Prince Harry and his bride, the former Meghan Markle. This gorgeous, intelligent and compassionate woman was one thing to the British media: half black. The American media also seemed fixated on that, but the British media's coverage was so extreme that five months after he began dating her, Harry authorized an official Royal statement condemning the racist and sexist reports that produced a swarm of ugly, vicious comments on social media.

Even after a fittingly glorious royal wedding, that continued. And it's safe to say the constant invasion of privacy (remember Prince Harry's mother and the press?) and racially toned invective of media reports was a chief underlying reason why the couple decided to vacate the royal family last year.

So, I am not looking at British society through non-colored glasses. However, living there provided a closer, in-depth opportunity to observe and participate in British life not distorted through a media lens; and I saw a country whose people had a far more open focus on race—including the reality of the one thing that seemed to send that media into a frenzy: interracial relationships.

Even the stately BBC network was guilty of that, as Madeline Morris said in a Tweet:

"The BBC keeps repeating the phrase 'modern couple' in reference to Harry and Meghan.

Which has to be code for the fact that Ms. Markle is mixed race.

Unlike the racial focus of the British media on Harry and Meghan's "modern couple" status, the portrayals of race in the British entertainment media were revelatory to me. I watched women of color play the heroine in adventure films, the leading lady in love stories, and the villain in dramas. They were romanced on television and billboard advertisements. Through all this, one could never assume the ethnicity of their male counterparts.

It stunned and delighted me. At last, I was seeing my reality reflected through the images I was seeing. I cannot tell you how rare that was for me growing up; finally, I was able to enjoy television instead of cringing as I waited for the next racial stereotype to rear its ugly head. But it never did. At last, I could see that "Happy Days" weren't just for white people.

(On a side note, something that really surprised me was the number of major television channels that featured synchronized sign language. I can only recall a rare few times I have seen sign language interpreters on American television shows, and these were mainly sponsored by the Public Broadcasting Service (PBS). If I felt ignored or stereotyped as an ethnic American, I can only imagine how downright invisible the deaf feel in America.)

It took me a little while to adjust to this refreshing and liberating perspective. But slowly I felt my mantle lifting and eventually I felt my spirit soaring freely in England, and I could be more open and honest in my social interactions. In a land 6,000 miles from my birthplace, I finally felt like I belonged in a way I never did in America. Quite simply, I felt accepted. I felt like me.

And my country began feeling a little stranger. Before my trip, even though I felt direct and indirect discrimination and prejudice, I truly believed that Americans were the leaders of diversity in the world.

I needed my experience in Britain to force a change in my belief regarding America and diversity. But it also led me to realize something else: that my dealing with uncomfortable racially infused situations with humor or biting my tongue in frustration was a form of deep denial and avoidance of societal/cultural issues.

My denial, I eventually realized, was my refusal to admit that America was not a champion of diversity. But my belief was so ingrained that I spent a great deal of time disbelieving the new social and cultural reality that surrounded me in British society. I did not expect such progressiveness. But when I finally embraced that people would accept me at face value, and I could do the same to them, it allowed me to relax and wholeheartedly immerse myself in the experience of enjoying how phenomenal it felt to be true to my true self.

As surprised as I was about my awakening, I was equally surprised about the British take on American cultural diversity. In the conversations with friends I made it was clear to me that many assumed their country was socially behind America in racial relations. It wasn't that they believed America had unequivocal racial equality; they just assumed that every American had the same chance to achieve the American dream.

While I do believe the American Dream is there for all, I also know that not everyone has an equal chance at it. When I told them there were many social inequities perpetuated by the American media and government that would be considered outrageous in the U.K., the reaction was always one of surprise.

That is when I understood that Great Britain – as far as racial acceptance and diversity – is what America pretends to be.

And nowhere is that more evident than the subject that this book is mostly about:

The hyphen.

# CHAPTER THREE

---

# THE HYPHEN

*"American means white, and Africanist people struggle to
make the term applicable to themselves with ethnicity and
hyphen after hyphen after hyphen."*

—Toni Morrison

N ow, I am not ignorant of the complexity of
the United Kingdom. Its four principal parts
--England, Northern Ireland, Scotland and
Wales—are proud of their rich regional identities. The
regions differ sharply on certain things—such as the 2016
Brexit vote when a majority of Scottish and Northern
Irish voted to stay with the European Union, with
England and Wales voting against.

But in December, 2020, when the time came to
make the final decision to either keep the pro-Brexit
Conservative Party in power or vote in the anti-Brexit

Labour Party, it was a conservative landslide. And I believe that is a testament not to how many Scots or Northern Irish had changed their minds in four years, but more of that stiff-upper-lip mentality of "if we're doing to this, let's do this and get on with it.

That is because when it finally comes down it, all Britons come together as one under the British flag. Some may prefer to be called English or Scottish, others as British. But no one refers to themselves as English-British, Irish-British, or Welsh-British.

Similarly, they never viewed me as anything other than what I am: an American. I immediately realized that in one of my first encounters, when a storekeeper asked if he could assist me. When I said yes, he responded, "Oh! You're an American!" I felt jolted for a moment as if reminded of something I had nearly forgotten. A strange sense of pride followed that in being called, only, an "American." To him, that is what I was. It was a startling moment of clarity. I realized this man did not view my ethnicity before my nationality.

And trust me, that small encounter says something huge about the difference between America and Britain, something my trip didn't teach me, but certainly solidified in my mind: the hyphenation of your nationality minimizes your standing in the nation. Grab a Sharpie and underline that sentence, circle it with a ballpoint pen, or highlight it on your Kindle, but that is what I most want you to realize in reading this book. The hyphen might as well be the symbol it most looks like: the minus sign — the same symbol, with the same consequences. Just as a minus "takes away" a numerical value, the hyphen lessens the value of your nationality.

I am not talking specifically about the .hyphen as a punctuation mark. I am talking about the subtext, the underlying meaning of the symbol that embodies the divisive concept that the term "hyphenated-American" connotes that there are many Americans who are "less than" or "other" Americans. It has nothing to do with that tiny, quite useful punctuation mar. Among its many functions, it the hyphen links, or glues, two or more words that come before a noun, in effect allowing them to act as a single idea modifying that noun.

But when it comes to people, the hyphen, or the concept it suggests, is far more injurious. And that concept applies to single-word labels, such as Hispanic and Latino and it will still apply even if the hyphen is banished altogether in terms of ethnicity and nationality, as the Associated Press, which is the Bible for most American media outlets in terms of style, announced in April 2019. It finally decided to get rid of the hyphen in referring to U.S. Citizens who are not white. Instead of African-American or Asian-American, AP Style now calls for African American and Asian American. That's great, but even without the hyphen, the term remains. As does the label.

Why is that a problem? Because even absent the hyphen, putting a person's ethnicity before their nationality still weighs heavily on the American psyche, for it all too often is used divisively to compartmentalize and marginalize.

Whether it's African-American or African American, Asian-American or Asian American, Hispanic or Latino or whatever, to live your life as a hyphenated American or with some other label thrust upon you is to not be put into a category with others that you may have something in common with; it is to be put into a box that separates you from those who, for whatever reason, need you to be separate. Instead of serving as a racial identifier of the colored tile in the so-called mosaic of America you belong to, it identifies you as something that doesn't quite belong in the picture of America that those with the real power have long seen as the real America. It is equivalent to saying, "Stay back! You are almost an American, but not completely, because of your ethnicity."

How shameful it is that in America I am categorized by my race first, nationality second? I am an American – period! I have had countless conversations with family and friends regarding this subject. Some believe the hyphen is a reminder of our cultural roots, of our African ancestors, kidnapped and forced into servitude, and that

African American honors them, and we should not sever that link. However, as I have never stepped foot on African soil, nor would an actual African ever think of me as African, why am I forced to accept the label?

And what is African anyway? Egypt is in Africa. So is Burkina-Faso, Morocco, Madagascar and the Democratic Republic of Congo. There are 54 countries on the continent, with 3,100 ethnic groups speaking more than 2,100 languages.

And what about people born in Africa of Caucasian ethnicity? Are they forced to call themselves "European-Africans" if they have never set foot in Europe? America is a nation of immigrants. Every person in America, excluding indigenous people, is the descendant of an immigrant who arrived here after 1500. The only people who are not compelled to hyphenate their nationality or adopt some other label that puts ethnicity before nationality are of Caucasian European descent. Does that make sense?

Yes, I genuinely believe that in terms of the opportunity to achieve dreams and be successful, America is unbeatable. But the hurdles people of color must overcome to make those dreams are beset with inequities that riddle most of our institutions, whether they are educational, political or economic.

And atop that list of inequities is the issue of identity, of self-determination. What is the toll on people who yearn and strive for their piece of the American dream, but who are considered not as Americans, but only partly Americans, the second part of that hyphenated term? At what point do they start believing that and acting, or not acting, accordingly?

It is my firm belief that the concept of the hyphenated American, of these labels that put a person's ethnicity before nationality, fosters the racial divide in this country. And doing away with that concept is vitally important in this nation fully recovering from the wounds it has carried since its inception, wounds that are a brazen contradiction to the idea that supposedly inspired it, of a country that is supposed to be one. Doubt that? Look at the words on our Great Seal, adopted in 1782: *E Pluribus Unum:* "Out of many, one."

So why are we so sharply divided? In the next two chapters, I hope to show you where the concept of the hyphenated American came from and how embedded it is in the very foundation of this country. And that makes this as good a time as any to introduce one of the pillars erected upon that foundation that helped support America's transformation into the world-striding colossus it is today. One of America's greatest presidents, and one who loathed the hyphen—but for reasons that may surprise some readers....

# CHAPTER FOUR

---

# PAST PRESIDENTIAL PERSPECTIVE

*"All the people like us are we, and everyone else is They."*

—Rudyard Kipling

Although he's one of the four presidents carved into Mt. Rushmore and one of the few who both Republicans and Democrats embrace, Theodore Roosevelt, the 26th president of the United States, is known as much for his garrulous, larger-than-life personality (President Barack Obama called him the "coolest" president ever) than his accomplishments in office.

But Roosevelt dominated the last years of the 19th Century and the first decade of the 20th, one of the most important eras in American history. Domestically, the country was transitioning from a nation of mostly rural residents into an industrialized society with an increasingly urbanized citizenry. Abroad, it was expanding its influence from the Philippines and Hawaii to Latin America, all made possible in large part by Roosevelt's insistence of an expanded U.S. Navy—and the "gunboat diplomacy" that expansion facilitated.

Roosevelt, who served as president from 1901-1908 and ran again in 1912 as a third-party candidate that split the Republican vote and gave Woodrow Wilson and the Democratic Party its first president not named Grover Cleveland in 52 years, was also the face of America during the time of its greatest wave of immigration. The "melting pot" was boiling, immigration was the most polarizing issue of the time and the use of hyphens to characterize Americans was one of its central battlegrounds.

And Roosevelt loathed the hyphen, which he felt was an international division of the races that undermined America.

In a 1915 Columbus Day speech, Roosevelt, who had not been president for six years but whose voice still carried clout, made his position clear:

*"There is no room in this country for hyphenated Americanism...a hyphenated American is not an American at all...The one absolutely certain way of bringing this nation to ruin...would be to permit it to become a tangle of squabbling nationalities, an intricate knot of German-*

*Americans, Irish-Americans, English-Americans, French-Americans, Scandinavian-Americans or Italian-Americans... each at heart feeling more sympathy with Europeans of that nationality than with the other citizens of the American Republic...There is no such thing as a hyphenated American who is a good American. The only man who is a good American is the man who is an American and nothing else."*

Modern conservatives often point to Roosevelt's speech, as well as words from his successor, Woodrow Wilson, as proof that the presidents during the most massive wave of immigration in U.S. history did not want a diverse, multicultural nation—even though both Roosevelt's and Wilson's opposition to the hyphen had more to do with fears about the impending war than diversification.

Roosevelt's audience was primarily Irish and German Catholics, many of whom sympathized with the plight of their native countries during World War I, which was currently raging in Europe. Roosevelt urged Americans to support intervention on the side of Britain and France. But Wilson, who would eventually make his 1916 campaign slogan "He Kept Us Out of War," wanted nothing to do with a European war—or with hyphenated Americans.

*'"Any man who carries a hyphen about with him carries a dagger that he is ready to plunge into the vitals of this Republic whenever he gets ready."*

However, while one supported intervention and the other didn't, the words of each show that by the mid-1910s, the term hyphenated American equated to disloyalty, treason, and betrayal.

It was a time of high anxiety, with opinion on entering the war, and who to support if America did enter, anything but united. And, like during many times of American insecurity, immigration played a key role. In 1910, the U.S. had a population of approximately 92 million, an increase of 21 percent from 1900, most of that fueled by the approximately 15 million who arrived here between 1900-1915, mostly from central or eastern Europe. Nearly 15 percent of the U.S. population was foreign-born in 1910.

Now consider that about 10 percent of the American population in 1910 had German roots, widely seen as the aggressor in the war, and New York City had more Irish than Dublin, and Ireland was having its problems with Great Britain. If America did enter the war, what side of the hyphen would these German-Americans and Irish-Americans and everything else-Americans support?

Roosevelt was very clear that he did not disapprove of naturalization and welcomed immigrants. He recognized that one did not need to be born on American soil to love and respect the country. (Clearly, some great shift has taken place in the many years since Roosevelt's words, since so many Americans not only view immigrants with suspicion but could not even accept an American-born black person as a full American!)

However, Roosevelt was adamant that immigrants fully assimilate into American society. In his 1894 essay, "What Does Americanism Mean," he wrote:

*"The third sense in which the word "Americanism" may be employed is with reference to the Americanizing of the newcomers to our shores... We welcome the German or the Irishman who becomes an American.... we want only Americans, and, provided they are such, we do not care whether they are of native or of Irish or of German ancestry... We have no room for any people who do not act and vote simply as Americans, and as nothing else."*

However, rather than fading away, as Roosevelt wished, the hyphen, or at least its concept, is more ubiquitous than ever. We may rarely hear the terms Irish American, Italian American or Polish American, but we certainly hear hyphenated words when it comes to people whose roots might lie in parts of the world where skin complexion is darker, whether it's African American, Arab American or Asian American.

Now, it is true that for many Americans from different ethnic backgrounds putting one's ethnicity before their nationality, or adopting an ethnic label, has become a proud source of identification for individuals and organizations. Just a few examples:

*National Association of Afro-American Artists.

*The Arab American Institute
*The Congressional Hispanic Caucus Institute
*Asian-American Government Executives Network
*Pakistani-American Association

I certainly take no issue with people organizing and standing together, nor all the good work organizations such as these and so many others have done. Claiming one's ethnicity is a way to celebrate and honor one's cultural and familial heritage, maintain one's group identity and to show, in the words of Stephen Covey, who wrote "7 Habits of Highly Effective People," that "strength lies in our differences, not our similarities."

But if you stop to think about it, I think it's hard not to ask one question: Why? Why do people from these groups feel the need to adopt these labels? It's because they were marginalized to begin with!

But many of us don't stop to question how the use of the hyphen, or, more importantly, the concept of the hyphenated American, may be directly influencing white Americans' attitudes towards people of color. Just consider its history.

The first use of hyphenated American came around 1889, but the concept stretches long before that. According to an article in the April 21, 2015, *New York Times,* the first documented use of a person's ethnicity before their American nationality was a 1782 advertisement in a Philadelphia newspaper for two sermons written by an "African American" preacher. Initially, putting ethnicity before nationality was not used derogatorily, but it became an epithet during the massive immigration wave of the late 19th and early 20th Century, a way to condemn anyone who called themselves anything other than American.

In an August 9, 1899, political cartoon in the magazine *Puck,* depicted a disgruntled Uncle Sam stood before a ballot box frowning disapprovingly as a line of people, all of whom had recently become naturalized, waited to cast their votes. The text read, "Why should I let these freaks cast whole ballots when they are only half Americans?"

By 1915, when Roosevelt gave his Columbus Day speech, and a war on the continent where so many new immigrants were from was raging, the term was seemingly on everybody's lips. No surprise, some 100 years later, when immigration is once again a polarizing topic in American society, separating people into ethnic categories in a way to cast doubt on how "American" they are, is once again in vogue.

Nowadays, some linguistic experts argue that using a hyphen before American is simply a way of indicating foreign ancestry, that any negative racial connotation is paranoid. The negative associations have long since been erased, they say, and hyphenating is merely a way of clarifying a person's heritage.

However, history tells a different story.

There was a time when many Americans did employ the term to differentiate between what they saw as "real" full-blooded Americans and the other. In 1914, a group of Americans formed a "Nordic supremacy" movement, which was headed by Madison Grant, whom some call the most influential nativist in American history.

Grant contended that a so-called Nordic race (which the Nazis called Aryans) was genetically superior. It's not worth going into his half-baked scientific and anthropological "proof" of this, which included racial cleansing through eugenics; His book, "The Passing of the Great Race," which claimed the U.S. would be destroyed by allowing immigrants of inferior genetic stock to overrun it, never sold that well popularly. But it was read and celebrated by many people in positions of influence, and some argue factored into the 1924 Immigration Act, which set quotas on immigrants from certain countries. Additionally, it was published in 1916, only a year after the second incarnation of the Ku Klux Klan formed, one that attempted to "re-brand" its hate in nativism and hostility to all immigrants. I can't help but wonder if the seeds of our contemporary white supremacist movements in the U.S. and Europe, were planted then.

If they were, that's a cruel irony. For one can argue that Roosevelt's doctrine of Americanism was designed to erase our differences, to bring all Americans together as Americans. If that is true, it has become distorted unimaginably since then. The concepts of Americanism and Nordic, or white, supremacy have become so intertwined at certain points in history that they are indistinguishable from one another, and today's white nationalists parrot that ideology by claiming that they are only protecting their 'ethnic heritage.'

A perfect example was the 2017 Unite the Right rally in Charlottesville, South Carolina, which included self-identified members of white supremacist groups. Met by counter-protesters, the rally turned hideously ugly, with more than 30 injuries and one death of a counter-protester after a member of a supremacist group rammed his car into a crowd.

Commenting on the ideological through-line between Grant's theories and today's white supremacists, *Atlantic* writer Adam Sewer said on NPR's "All Things Considered" on March 2019:

"We have to be extremely careful about disregarding the baseline American values that are, in my view, what makes this country a wonderful place to be, which is that anybody can come here and be an American. And we shouldn't define American citizenship on the basis of race and religion in the way that we once did."

However, some Americans do not share that opinion. On April 27, 2019, the same day that an admitted white supremacist opened fire on a Jewish synagogue in Poway,

California, killing one person and wounding three, a small group of white nationalists stormed an event in Washington D.C. for a book titled "Dying of Whiteness: How the Politics of Racial Resentment Is Killing America's Heartland." The irony of the latter small-scale incident would be almost comical if the former weren't so horrific.

We are a nation still seriously grappling with issues of race, which I think fuels much of the rhetoric around immigration. I don't think it's off-base to suggest that one reason for that is that more than 100 years after the concept of hyphenated Americans was at the heart of considerable debate over what a "real" American was, it still is. True, it's coding has changed: once denounced as a marker of disloyalty to America, now is used as a signifier, one that says clearly "you are different, no matter if you were born here or not."

But, and I know the following paragraphs will rile a few people up, the issue isn't confined to just racists using terms to separate Americans into "us vs. them" camps. Also contributing to the divide are those who willingly adopt the terms of racial difference in the belief they are doing their respective communities a disservice by not intentionally drawing attention to their race.

People of color are told that we must celebrate our uniqueness and our diversity, while simultaneously adopting a hyphenated name that does not necessarily speak to our own histories. By choosing to adopt terms that signal, to some, that we are less than American, are we perpetuating the racial divide in this country rather than bridging it?

Roosevelt wanted to bridge that divide and build a more cohesive America, but he did not get his wish. He did, however, make some accurate predictions and one provides a ray of hope even in these dark times.

In the spring of 1916, Roosevelt again discussed the hyphen, in a speech given to an audience in St. Louis, Missouri. However, this time, he spoke of the future:

*"The children and children's children of all of us have to live here in this land together. Our children's children will intermarry, one with another, your children's children, friends, and mine. They will be the citizens of one country. Even if they wished, they could not remain citizens of foreign countries...*

He was correct in assuming that the U.S. would become a multicultural nation, and the descendants of many people in his audience today live in multicultural households or are in interracial relationships. That will no doubt continue, as the younger generations of Americans don't seem as locked into the rigid mindset that interracial relationships are unusual.

But another passage in the speech mentioned above is more ominous.

*The effort to keep our citizenship divided against itself by the use of hyphen and along the lines of national origin is certain to breed a spirit of bitterness and prejudice and dislike between great bodies of our citizens."*

Roosevelt certainly did not want that, but that is what we have. For what he failed to predict was how the term hyphenated American would change over a century, from "someone with divided loyalties" to "someone different than you." This is an important distinction to make and a chief reason why people of color are often viewed as outsiders even if their families have been here for generations.

For example, in certain parts of the country, such as southern California, Hispanics have raised families for generations, and yet are still frequently viewed as outsiders. One reason for that, and why so many people of color are still regarded as second-class citizens, is that we have been given, or I should say, we have had thrust upon us, a particular designation in order to remind us, and certain elements of white America, that we are less than real Americans. That we should be distrusted solely for the color of our skin and not the legitimacy of our birth certificates. That we will never live up to the standards of the ideal American—that is to say, a white American.

For evidence, look at our current polarized view of immigration. President Trump wants to build a wall along our southern border to keep brown people out, but he doesn't seem too concerned about building a northern wall to keep Canadians out. My main question over immigration is whether white Americans fear immigration as a whole or merely a certain kind of immigration?

Near the end of that May 1916 speech, Roosevelt described his personal experiences with naturalized citizens and immigrants who became proud to be Americans:

*"Here in this city I could repeat name after name of men of German birth who as American citizens have had distinguished records of intense loyalty to the Union, [...] and as patriots."*

The same could be said about millions of American today who are of non-European heritage. They are as American as the flag, and many have shed blood defending it and will continue to do. However, the reality is most likely you have friends, neighbors, and colleagues who are those kinds of Americans but who, in the back of their minds, thanks to the labels affixed to them, are constantly reminded that they are different, that they will never be viewed as full Americans, no matter what their personal experiences may be.

Having now lived in the U.K. as well as the U.S., one a country where the hyphen, and its divisive *otherness,* is unnecessary, the other where it specifies or muddies, the definition of its citizens, I would love to see Americans begin to make a step towards removing it entirely from not only our vernacular but from our minds.

But to do that we will need to correct something written into the DNA of America.

# CHAPTER FIVE

---

# CONSTITUTIONAL CONSIDERATIONS

*"I would not look to the U.S. Constitution if
I were drafting a constitution in 2012."*

—Ruth Bader Ginsberg

A s I wrote earlier, I am a proud, patriotic American who loves my country and thinks, at our best, we are the greatest ever to exist. But I also think every American, particularly those who most claim to love it, needs to honestly study and confront those times when America has failed to live up to its lofty ideals. Only in considering the best, and worst, of anything, do we begin to get a full measure of what it is, and how we can make it better.

And making it better is why I wrote this book.

The impetus was my eye-opening experience in Great Britain when I realized how race, or ethnicity, is used to separate Americans rather than bring them together. Before that trip, I knew race remained a factor in America; my mantle was enough to remind me of that. But I also thought the notion of race, and racism, was fading; that the successes of our history—the ending of slavery, the eradication of "separate but equal" and Jim Crow, the Civil Rights Movement-- showed that, as Rev. King said (quoting a 19th Century preacher) that while the moral arc of the universe is long, it always bends toward justice.

But after that trip, I wrestled with a dichotomy that I had sensed as a young girl but never looked at seriously. That was the disconnect between the stirring words in our founding documents, such as "all men are created equal," and "life, liberty and the pursuit of happiness, and in our ceremonial rituals, the Pledge of Allegiance's "with liberty and justice for all," the National Anthem's "land of the free and home of the brave," contrasted against historical reality, one in which so many times we have fallen short of those ideals. How could a nation founded on those ideas even need a Civil War and a Civil Rights movement to end practices that seemed so fundamentally against its character?

In my search for answers, I knew I needed to start with our nation's birth. As fortune would have it, an opportunity to study that historic event came when I enrolled in an online constitutional law class at Yale University. There I learned that the seeds of racial divisiveness besieging contemporary America are literally written into the documents that our country is based upon.

Before the class, I had a cursory knowledge of the U.S. Constitution. But I didn't realize that our standing constitution was America's second, based in large part on The Articles of Confederation, which were ratified in 1781 and served as the law of the land until 1789. Nor did I realize both sprang to life in the context of racial subjugation, and the writers of each made sure to include language to perpetuate that subjugation, namely that people of African descent who were kidnapped and subjected to a nightmarish passage across the Atlantic were not human beings, but mere property.

I still believe the Constitution is the most well-written and well-conceived document in the history of democracy. Nevertheless, after countless hours of studying its intricacies, and numerous conversations with my colleagues, I came to realize slavery was the fundamental issue in the drafting, and *signing,* of the Constitution. I based this conclusion on three distinct premises: The Three-Fifths Compromise; the specific verbiage written within the Articles of Confederation; and the number of slave owners who helped to frame, create and sign the Constitution.

First, the Three-Fifths Compromise, perhaps the most critical step in ensuring the Constitution's ratification. The Articles of Confederation apportioned each state's number of representatives and its electoral votes based on land value, with slaves counting only in how much value they added to that property. The Three-Fifths Compromise based the number of representatives and votes on the number of people living in a state. But who was a person? Northern delegates wanted only free persons counted; but since the majority of the population lived in the northern states, southern delegates pushed for slaves to count as people. After a contentious debate, the compromise was finally reached to count slaves as three-fifths of a person, giving the southern states about a third more representatives and electoral votes.

The compromise had three significant consequences: it ensured that enough states would sign the Constitution; it gave the South much more voting power (four of America's first five presidents, and nine of the first 11, were from southern states); and it wrote into the very document that defined America and from where all law flowed that the buying, selling and breeding of men and women of African descent was not only condoned and lucrative but also good for the state in which one lived.

This was a blatant contradiction to "all men are created equal." If anything, it was more "all men are created equal, but some are far more equal than others." And those men were white men, particularly if they owned other human beings.

Of course, considering its source, how could anyone be shocked that the U.S. Constitution perpetuated, and even rewarded, America's Original Sin? Just consider the Articles of Confederation, a document that clearly stated it was exclusively written for the benefit of white inhabitants:

*"To borrow money or emit bills on the credit of the United States to build and equip a navy; to agree upon the number of land forces; and to make requisitions from each State for its quota, in proportion to the number of **white** inhabitants in such State."* (Emphasis mine. This document is housed at the Lillian Goldman Law Library at Yale Law School.)

The Articles of Confederation were drafted six years *after* the commencement of the American Revolutionary War. They were signed even though black and white men had fought, and *at that time,* were still fighting and dying, side by side, for the freedom of all Americans until the war's end two years later, in 1783. America may have been a new country, but it had no problem benefiting from its old colonial master's business model.

Finally, let's look at the signers of the Constitution. When it came time to ratify the document, 38 of 41 delegates signed. An examination of those Founding Fathers reveals that about a third could also be called Founding Slave Owners as 11 of the 38 owned slaves at the time they signed the Constitution. I do not believe it is too much of a stretch to think that slave owners wanted to protect their interests and investments.

In conclusion – and yes, I am loath to write this, but unable to make any other deduction – not only was the Constitution pro-slavery, but its exclusionary principles became the moral and judicial foundation of our country. And, oh, how quickly that foundation was built upon. A mere two years after the Constitution took effect, Congress passed the Naturalization Act of 1790, which gave citizenship to anyone who had resided two years in the U.S. Any person, that is, who was "free" and "white." (Yes, even free white women could naturalize after two years, but it took them a little while to become full citizens and earn the right the vote: like 130 years.)

Some would argue that the mistakes of the Founding Fathers were righted by the addition of the Bill of Rights, as well as subsequent amendments and landmark U.S. Supreme Court decisions. But while the first 10 amendments in the Bill of Rights came two years after the Constitution's implementation, everything else came far later, and there were plenty of laws passed, and Supreme Court decisions, that reinforced those exclusionary words.

Remember, it took the bloodiest war in this country, where we literally fought ourselves, and 76 years after the Constitution was ratified to make slavery illegal (the 13th Amendment, in 1865), and three years *after* that for former slaves to become citizens (the 14th Amendment). But it still wasn't enough. In 1870, the passage of the 15th Amendment ensured that a person's race could not be used as a criterion for voting, even though the only word in the Constitution to refer to Americans was citizen, so why race would still be a hindrance after former slaves were citizens is a question not even our professor could answer. Clearly, the American government had violated its own Constitution. And it still was 94 years later, as after the failed experiment of Reconstruction allowed Jim Crow to flourish and Southern states put up one obstacle after another to prevent black people from voting, the 24th Amendment passed, abolishing the anti-poor discriminatory poll tax.

To put it all in perspective, from the Constitution's becoming the law of the land in 1789 to the 24th Amendment in 1967, the federal and state governments were in direct violation of that very document for *178 years*. Thomas Jefferson's foresight was profound when he surmised, "*The Constitution, on this hypothesis, is a mere thing of wax in the hands of the Judiciary, which they may twist and shape into any form they please."*

And while overt barriers are gone, problems persist. In 2018, a survey by *The Atlantic* and the Public Religion Research Institute showed that suppression of black and Hispanic voters was widespread, with 9 percent of those respondents saying they were told they lacked the proper identification to vote (compared to 3 percent of white respondents) and over 10.5 percent of black and Hispanics were incorrectly told they were not on the voter rolls, twice as many as white respondents.

It took this lesson on the Constitution for me to finally appreciate the importance of understanding my history. I now understand how the cage of institutionalized racism has trapped Congress from its birth. Of course, considering that historically Congress has been dominated by older, white men, implicit biases may also have contributed to that shameful legacy.

I know what some of you are thinking: our current Congress is the most diverse yet, for the fifth consecutive time. Yes, the 116th Congress inaugurated in January 2019 included 25 women senators and 102 representatives, accounting for nearly 25 percent of Congress. These included the first two Muslim and first two Native American women to serve in Congress, Massachusetts and Connecticut's first two African American women, and the youngest woman to ever serve in congressional history, 29-year-old Alexandria Ocasio-Cortez. Ethnically? There were 56 Black members, 44 Hispanic or Latino, 17 Asian and four Native Americans. That means 22 percent of Congress is non-white, a marked difference from 1945 when the total was just 1 percent.

But the reality is that Congress still has a long way to go: the number of non-whites in America is 39 percent, or 17 percent more than the Congressional representation. And women make up 51 percent of the country, more than twice the number of women in Congress. Yes, we're making progress and, yes, we've come a long way, but that it isn't enough. The foundation of this country, our very Constitution rests on sand: the precept that we are not a racially homogenous nation. Until Americans confront the blemishes of our history and confront them; and until we demand more than just a facelift in Congress but an entirely different mindset when it comes to race and who is a "real" American, we will continue to repeat and reinforce the practice of inequality that renders nearly half of our citizens as something other than genuine Americans.

The U.S. Constitution is a remarkable and inspiring document. On the page. But the subtext beneath those glowing words, and its interpretation for much of our history, shows it can be manipulated to further racial divisiveness and suit the desires and objectives of the status quo. For a very recent example, look at the June

2019 Supreme Court case in which the five conservative-leaning justices voted that federal judges have no power to stop state politicians from drawing electoral districts to preserve or even strengthen their party's control. That process, called gerrymandering, is one key reason why minority representation in the House has been so historically low; when politicians can redraw boundaries in bizarrely shaped ways to limit the number of minorities in those districts, the numerical odds are stacked against minority candidates. This seems to undermine both the Voting Rights of 1965, which made it illegal to draw districts that intentionally dilute the voting power of minorities, as well as the 14th Amendment's equal protection clause, in terms of equal representation and, as justice Elena Kagen said in her dissent, the concept of "free and fair elections."

Until Americans make an effort to raise their collective consciousness and pay attention to whom we have elected to guide our country's future, there will always be a governmental effort to control the opinion of the majority concerning racial respect and cultural diversity. Each of us as American citizens must take the time to study and understand our nation's Constitution. The individuals who take the time to learn about the past are the ones who will ultimately shape our future.

The images of equality and nationalism we represent to the world via the media are false. The foundation of our own Constitution is different from what we practice. These same leaders who claim to espouse the lofty principles of the Founding Fathers have assisted in reinforcing a divisive mindset via the hyphenation of American citizens.

Putting *all* Americans on an equal footing is a good start to correcting that. And maybe that begins with ridding the hyphen, and the labels that it creates, as a tool to separate Americans into different categories of authenticity. That would, at the very least, be one step closer to embodying the stirring first three words of the Constitution. Need a reminder? Look at the first three words of our Constitution:

WE THE PEOPLE

# CHAPTER SIX

# NOTES ON THE ENGLISH LANGUAGE

*We cannot control the way people interpret our ideas or thoughts, but we can control the words and tones we choose to convey them....one wrong word, or misinterpreted word, can change the meaning of an entire sentence and start a war. And one right word, or one kind word, can grant you the heavens and open doors."*

—Suzy Kassem

**W**ords are powerful. They can inspire, empower and provide meaning and context. But they can also wound, scar and rob people of their significance. And for too long in this country, the words used to describe Americans as dictated by the white power structure have done the latter. That's why it's so essential for those of us outside that power structure to give ourselves power by claiming our own words, from the ones that most define us, to those we use in simple conversation.

But when it comes to words, many people of color, particularly black Americans, are hurting their cause, duplicating the linguistic and identity transgressions they have suffered since this country's formation. Since the first U.S. Census in 1790, people of African descent have seen the following boxes on the census form to check for race: slave, free colored, black, mulatto, quadroon, octoroon, negro, African American.

Conversely, since 1790, Caucasian Americans have had one box: white. Is it any wonder that many black individuals have difficulty defining who they are, and what they want to be labeled? Or why someone like me, who does not define myself by skin hue, grows so weary of continually being asked by white Americans whether I prefer to be called black or African-American? I have no preference because neither defines who I am. I'm just Nicole, another American just like you.

For more than 200 years, identities of far too many Americans have been defined by words chosen by others. Imagine if that were you. How could you possibly know for sure *who* you are when someone else has been telling you all your lives *what* you are?

I feel that is why black people in this country have primarily adopted the term African American. By choosing to identify with a word that they wanted, rather than being stuck with a label someone else put on them, they feel some semblance of self-empowerment. But in selecting a term they think better symbolizes their identity other than their skin color, they are also placing the name of a continent they most likely know very little about it front of their American nationality. I wonder if they are repeating the same pattern as those who were identified by truly obnoxious terms like colored, negro and "oppressed Americans." By pointing out the differences they have with other Americans, are they feeding into a system that somehow benefits from the misguided notion that there are tangible differences between Americans?

But at least African American is a word chosen by the black community. That's not the case with another word that seems increasingly in vogue these days: the n-word. It doesn't take a psychoanalyst to realize that those who wield that word carry a great deal of pain and repressed anger. And I am not talking just about the racists who use it; I mean anyone who uses it, including black people who find some sort of reverse justice in its use. But the same hurt and anger are at work, and to shield against that, many blacks have decided to follow the infinite wisdom of whoever said, "Hey, let me take this word and turn it into something less painful. Let's call our friends and family members that word in an affectionate manner. Let's call *ourselves* that word."

I vividly remember the reaction of my grandparents, along with many others, in the 1970s when a word freighted with the history of so much brutality and oppression became a form of endearment among the same people who had suffered so much. They bristled at that, and I don't blame them. Instead of rejecting the word altogether, and defining themselves in an entirely new way, too many black people have made it acceptable by accepting and using it, even finding some measure of self-respect in what they think is owning it.

Have they forgotten that for centuries this word existed to call attention to what many Americans needed to believe: the inferior nature of blacks? The thought that there is some vindication in people using that word, that it somehow erases all its history seems ludicrous to me, as does identifying with a word that so long defined you and yours negatively.

If I call you a name that cuts you to your core, and you accept and adopt it and think you have turned the tables by now owning it, I must ask, "Who emerged victoriously?" Take a moment to ask yourself this: how "Do *I* define myself? Or have I allowed *someone else* to define me?"

In 2008, Arizona State University humanities professor Neal A. Lester taught the first college-level course explicitly focused on examining the n-word. The reason the class was necessary, he told <u>www.tolerance.org</u> was that:

"It's about self-education and self-critique, not trying to control others by telling them what to say or how to think, but rather trying to figure out how we think and how the words we use mirror our thinking."

And speaking of words mirroring, or not mirroring, our thinking, I have to bring up a pet peeve of mine: Ebonics.

The ability to communicate articulately, to speak grammatically correct English, is a key to opportunity in America. It is alarming that although English is the primary language taught in American schools, so many speak it so poorly. The fact that someone can come to America from a non-English speaking country and after a few classes speak the English language with more alacrity than many native speakers who have spoken and heard it almost exclusively their entire lives is a travesty. If you only know one language, yet speak it poorly, is it wrong for society in general to question your intelligence?

That is why I was so disheartened by the controversy in the mid-1990s over an Oakland school district's announcement to consider Ebonics a second language for black students. Ebonics was coined in 1973 as a term for African American Vernacular English, a dialect spoken in many black communities that has its roots in the ways that former slaves communicated with one another.

While some linguists claim that it a historically significant dialect and worthy of respect, I find that notion repellant in 20th Century America. In a standard English dictionary, there is only one correct way to pronounce most English words. Yes, there are intonations and variations, but the basic pronunciation remains the same. I can't tell you how many times I have seen or heard a black person admonish another who tries to speak correctly saying, in so many words: "You just want to sound like you are white." I find that extremely disturbing and pejorative, considering all the speaker is doing is clearly speaking to be understood.

There is no *berfday*, but there *is* a birthday. You cannot *ax* a question; however, you can ask a question. When you do not take the time to articulate the only language you speak correctly, you may have to accept it when your intelligence is questioned.

I have heard some maintain that speaking Ebonics is a sign of respect for those of African descent who did not have access to proper education and had to synthesize their version of English to communicate with other slaves. By using this lazy and nonsensical way of speaking, they are "keeping it real." They sure are: They are "keeping it *really* stupid."

The reality is, you are instantly judged by the way you communicate. The message you bring, regardless of content, is immediately discounted if you can't articulate the words.

Language is usually learned from the parents. However, since not all parents (both native and non-native English speakers) communicate the English language correctly, poor grammar has become a legacy. In school, some teachers speak grammatically incorrect English as well. What chance does a child have, when neither parent nor teacher can speak English properly? If young people aren't taught to speak English correctly, to communicate at the simplest level, how can they ever hope to understand it, and how can they not see that the words others use, and which they adopt, further their marginalization and otherness?

We don't hear much about Ebonics these days. But I don't think that is because it's no longer used. I think it's been relegated to the back burner because the government-run educational system has quietly accepted it as a fact of life. Instead of mandating that elocution be part of the grade school curriculum, they have allowed poor English to become the standard, which makes no sense to me.

Elocution classes should start as early as preschool and be mandatory until the child has mastered enunciation of the English language Perfectly spoken and written

English should be the standard, *not* the exception. A mandatory elocution test should be required for all teachers as well. How can a teacher help a student to achieve success if they can't communicate articulately?

This goal is neither impossible nor improbable. It is imperative Americans of all ethnicities stand together and say no more. Until we are capable of genuine communication—and that includes the actual use of words as well as their intent and meaning—how can we resolve social inequities? If you were born in America, but can't speak the language, how can you comprehend it—and why should anybody take you seriously as an American? The passive acceptance of an inferior mode of communication by an ethnic group helps foster the racial divide in this country. Those who cannot adequately articulate the language are merely reinforcing the biases of those who need to believe there are certain types of people incapable of mastering American English and therefore are not full, "real" Americans.

And to those who say Ebonics or street-level black speech is somehow more liberating or honest because it is *our* way of speaking, this is how *we* communicate, and it somehow honors our imprisoned ancestors who developed it as a way to communicate? Well, it's not *my* way of speaking. It's not how *I* communicate. And I wrote a book.

Not that I would ever dream of being mentioned anywhere close to the following people, but ask yourself this: how successful in their chosen endeavors, how inspiring and memorable, would the following people have been had they *not* learned and practiced simple elocution? And then ask yourself, how can anyone inspire like these figures *without* knowing how to speak well?

Martin Luther King. Barack Obama, Maya Angelou. Malcolm X. Myrlie Evers-Williams. Carl T. Rowan. Kweisi Mfume. Colin Powell.

Word.

# CHAPTER SEVEN

---

# RAINBOW OF ETHNICITIES

*"Change the way you look at things,
and the things you look at change."*

—Wayne W. Dyer

A s I've pointed out in the previous four chapters, words are effective instruments in helping to articulate the misguided notion that there are some Americans who are fully 100 percent American, and those who are not. But images, or, I should say, our perception of images, are perhaps more effective. Regardless of how distorted, untruthful or ridiculous as they may seem, images often feel more real than reality itself. And that is why it so important to change the way we look at those images because they play such a significant role in how we look at each other and ourselves.

I know it's a broad generalization, but I am convinced that every person of color in America has at some point felt a spotlight focusing on them, not for the person they are, but for the color of their skin. How many times have you seen a new kid in class, a new person at work, a new employee at your local Starbucks, who looks different than the rest of the group? And the questions and assumptions come: Where are you from? What is your race? What country were you born in? No, those aren't racist questions, and there is nothing wrong with curiosity, but ask yourself this; when is the last time you saw a new white person in a group peppered with the same inquiries? Unless they speak with a noticeable accent, they won't be. Because their skin color isn't *assumed* to make them exotic, or different, regardless of how long they and their families have lived in America.

If no words were spoken and I stood next to a Scandinavian person visiting the U.S., he or she would have a much better chance of being assumed to be American than myself, even though I was born and raised in America. This is just another way how the construct of race and our willing adoption of it separates Americans into real and not-so-real camps.

Compounding the issue is that people of color so often do it to ourselves.

Actresses Halle Berry, Rashida Jones and Tracee Ellis Ross are three black Americans I can think off the top of my head who drew criticism for refusing to embrace any part of their heritage that wasn't African, as if any other blood in their veins was unimportant. In 2018, two actors in the film "Crazy Rich Asians" were criticized for playing Asian characters when they were only half-Asian. This type of internal prejudice within a community can only hurt the struggle for acceptance of diversity, rather than aid it.

I have felt it personally. I spent a great deal of my younger years either visiting relatives or living in Irvine, an affluent city in Orange County, California. I can't tell you how often I was asked by my darker-skinned friends how I could live in what was then an overwhelmingly white city. They could not believe that I did not feel ostracized or at least uncomfortable being one of the few people with black skin who lived there. But the reality was I didn't feel uncomfortable at all; it was quiet, peaceful, people were friendly, and I never felt different—unless someone asked me about it. I understand why those who were not raised in an ethnically diverse environment, as I was, could feel awkward or singled out, but I never did.

Neither did race affect who I dated. I dated who I liked, plain and simple. Fortunately, I had parents who viewed my dating choices similarly: as long as the boy was intelligent and treated me well, he could have been a Martian for all they cared. It was black men who had issues with me dating outside of my race. Invariably, one would feel compelled to lecture me on how confused I must be since I didn't know my people's history. That argument always felt weak to me; I have always known who I am, and my history, and I knew that dating someone outside of my ethnicity was not a betrayal to my race but a living example of tolerance and respect and promotes social progress.

If members of ethnic minorities are expected to both prove their loyalty to their race and conveniently fit into the box that others have picked for them, where do these impossible racial stereotypes and double binds leave Americans who may claim many different ethnicities all at once, or who may not want ethnicity to define them at all? Sadly, it doesn't matter. Because in America, there is an enormous elephant in the room, and that elephant is white. Yes, the part of the world where you or your ancestors came from, your ethnic heritage, defines your status as an American, but the most significant part of that definition is the actual color of your skin. And the closer that color comes to the hue of what an American *should* look like, the closer you are to American.

It's an absurd notion if you think about it since American is a nationality, not an ethnicity. But after much research on this subject, I believe that physical appearance is, by and large, how Americans view what a real American is. And I am sad to report that in 2020 a real American is still perceived by many, particularly those in power, as a white American. That is as damaging to the psyche of American people of color as the identity-crippling and marginalizing concept of the hyphen. And it far more damaging physically and perhaps even mentally.

The idealized look of an American is closely tied into the standard of beauty this country has chosen to adopt, the Northern European standard: fair skin, straight hair, slim and statuesque. Yes, curves periodically make a comeback but turn on your TV or open a magazine, and you're still going to see the vast majority of so-called beautiful women tending toward the thinner side of the spectrum, even if their breasts tend to be disproportionately larger than that type. And those women tend to be white, or, if they have a darker shade, it's very light.

And then there's the hair.

Why has it taken SO long for the "natural hair movement" to finally gain legal standing? Black women, along with many other women of color, in this country have long labored under the constraints of "ideal" beauty, and have subjected themselves to countless hours of follicle torture by trying to straighten their naturally curly hair. In effect, they have felt compelled to alter one of the most personal physical characteristics of any woman, their hair, because it doesn't fit into the conventional view of feminine beauty equating with straight, usually long, hair of the European ideal. So many women have been mistreated because of the texture of their hair, particularly in the workplace, and how it was deemed "unprofessional." Many with styles such as dreadlocks, braids, cornrows and twists were fired or otherwise disciplined, and many black girls in high school are disciplined for daring to wear a non-conventional (in terms of straight white people hair) style.

But in June 2019, California Governor Gavin Newsom signed a bill banning hair discrimination targeting hairstyles associated with race, making California the first to put it into law. The language of the bill alludes to one of my contentions in this book

"In a society in which hair has historically been one of many determining factors of a person's race, and whether they were a second-class citizen, hair today remains a proxy for race," the bill says. "Therefore, hair discrimination targeting hairstyles associated with race is racial discrimination."

It is far past time for a leading state like California to recognize this affront to personal choice. No one, regardless of race, religion or anything else, should be discriminated against because of how they choose to wear their hair. Hopefully, it is the first step toward a broader and more inclusive standard of beauty being embraced.

But that is an uphill struggle. The Eurocentric concept of beauty, with one of its foremost peddlers the American media, is now the global standard. Look at Spanish-language *telenovelas,* where the heroines all have blonde hair, and the villains are always the darker shades of brown. Or, the global demand of skin-whiteners, estimated by Global Industry Analysts to climb to $31.2 billion by 2024, almost double the $17.9 billion in 2017.

The reality is that women of diverse heritages come in all shades, and many Americans of color are a combination of different ethnicities. All you have to do is walk down any street of any big city in America, and you're going to realize that beautiful looking women (it is only skin deep, remember) are not limited to one particular ideal. But the fact is that Americans refuse to acknowledge that race and ethnicity are not synonymous. Many Americans seem to mix them up, along with nationality.

While some argue that race is a construct and that there is no determined arrangement of genes that comprise race, I am talking about the conventional way of classifying people on physical and biological attributes, such as hair and eye color, bone structure and skin color. There are only four major races: Caucasia (primarily Europe and the Middle East) (Negroid (black, mostly Africa); Mongoloid (eastern Asia), Australoid (South East Asia, Oceania).

Ethnicity is belonging to the same social group and is determined more by culture, such as a common language, ancestry, food, art or language. There are thousands of ethnicities (Nigeria alone has 250) and, like race, members of ethnic groups can be spread across the world, such as Jews. You cannot choose your race, though some try, and while I suppose you can select your ethnicity, it's' difficult. But nationality is entirely different. That's a legal definition, the relationship a person has with the state in which they are a citizen.

The irony is that even though minority women are basically excluded from any conversation about conventional beauty, (unless their features, hair and bodies reflect the white European standard) they are also blasted by other members of their community when they are comfortable enough in their own skin not to proclaim that they are solely one ethnicity.

An excellent example of this was the controversy regarding Beyoncé Knowles' L'Oréal TV commercial. In the ad, she said: "There's a story behind my skin. It is a mosaic of all the faces before it. My only makeup? True Match." She was described in the commercial as African American, Native American, and French, and the combination created her skin tone. The ad provoked a backlash throughout the black online community, with many arguing that she should have said she was 100% African American just like Jennifer Lopez, whose own ad stated she was 100% Puerto Rican. Some suggested the L'Oréal ads whitewashed Beyoncé's skin and some claimed she was denying her ties to the black community, which played the most prominent part in making her a star.

The British paper *The Daily Mail* reported: "Some commentators have expressed fears that these images of the superstar singer — who is famous for her honey-toned hair and complexion — could have the effect of making darker-skinned black girls ashamed of how they look..."

Due to fame and popularity, Beyoncé is a role model. But I cannot comprehend how she or the hue of her skin can be held responsible for the effects of a commercial on others' self-esteem. This is especially true when you are the product of a multi-racial heritage. The fact that you are brown does not negate the other ethnicities that have contributed to your personal history. That is like suggesting Taylor Swift should never be anything but blonde and pale because if she tanned and dyed her hair black, the self- esteem of pale-skinned children would suffer. If a picture of a black celebrity who has been Photoshopped to appear lighter is all it takes to make a darker-skinned girl ashamed of how she looks, that is a sad testament to the pride and dignity instilled in our young children.

(However, I should add that I do not want to come across as negating the effects of colorism and how children, regardless of their skin color, are extremely susceptible to what they see around them and in the media. Because of the Eurocentric standards of beauty that exist globally, I want to acknowledge that the effects of these standards and colorism contribute to the self-esteem of darker-skinned girls, even though this SHOULDN'T even be a THING anymore.)

And those children grow into adults.

Recently I was at dinner with a group of friends, and part of a conversation that blew me away. Within this conversation, one person said, "Even though I am attracted to (a certain person), I would never date them because we are different ethnicities, and I think we would clash culturally." I wondered how they could clash culturally when they grew up in the same neighborhood, went to the same school and church, and generally were within the same circle of friends. The only difference between them was their ethnicity.

The dual perception that a person's ethnicity most defines who they are and that having a different skin hue automatically makes them culturally different is a change long overdue in this country. But that shift in awareness won't be easy. We have personal and collective histories to overcome. And, as I examine in the next chapter, we live in an era where image still reigns supreme, and where the primary disseminator of the image of the American identity continues to wield enormous influence.

# CHAPTER EIGHT

---

# STEREOTYPES AND THE AMERICAN MEDIA

*"We must reject not only the stereotypes*
*that others hold of us, but also the*
*stereotypes that we hold of ourselves."*
*—Shirley Chisholm*

L ike most young children with a mind absorbing everything, my favorite questions, the ones I'm curious never drew my parents insane, always began with why?

*Why is the sky blue?*

*Why is water wet?*

*Why do dogs have tails?*

My parents did their best, answering those questions they could, humoring me when they couldn't, ignoring the really bizarre ones. However, when I entered middle school, I became less curious about the big world around me and more curious about the smaller one in front of me. *Why during lunch did kids tend to sit with others who looked like them? Why, if I wanted to join a particular club, did my friends of color ask why I'd want to be a member of a group with no black people?*

Around the same time, I stopped passively absorbing the media stimuli that I devoured up to that point and began looking at it differently.

And my questions began changing:

*Why are so few superheroes depicted as people of color? Why are couples on television always the same ethnicity? Why are there so many negative portrayals of minorities on television?*

As a middle-class young person of color, I yearned for a television show that depicted a family somewhat like my own. But the only shows I remember with black leading actors featured them surrounded by poverty and speaking like they hadn't passed the eighth grade. I may have laughed at the antics of the characters on "Good Times" and "Sanford and Son," but I rarely related to their experiences.

In my juvenile mind, being "poor" equated to not getting what I wanted when I wanted it. I had no real concept of it in my real life—except when I visited some friends' houses, some of them white, and saw sparsely furnished, disorderly houses, bare cupboards, old clothes, and absent parents. This was the reality I witnessed growing up. My family was extremely comfortable in comparison.

But then something happened like a gift from high: Sept. 2, 1984, the premiere episode of "The Cosby Show."

Without minimizing or negating show creator Bill Cosby's conviction, I can say that "The Cosby Show" was like a dream come true.

In my house, that first episode was like the Super Bowl. We sat around the TV an hour ahead of time, and it did not disappoint. It was like watching an alternate version of my own family. The Huxtables spoke, dressed, and confronted the same everyday issues as my family. Most importantly, they *looked* like my family. I remember my sisters and I patterning our outfits based on what the show's children wore. Ironically, many of my friends said our family was very much like the Cosby family. I wore that compliment like a medal of pride.

However, though every week a new "Cosby Show" aired felt like a holiday for my family, not everyone shared my joy. I heard people discussing how "real" the TV family was, considering the disparity between the Huxtables' upscale lifestyle and the assumed lifestyles of black/minority families. People wondered whether the show felt like a slap in the face to people of color because they knew that TV reality was unattainable.

Many times, strangers, usually Caucasian, would ask me what I felt about the show, usually prefaced with a statement about how I must love it. I know now they weren't genuinely interested in my opinion because they worked for Nielsen; they never asked what I thought about "Cheers" or "The A Team" or "Murder She Wrote." It was more like they couldn't connect with me, a young black female, on any other level but that show. Their interest had less to do with the program's impact on me, than its impact on *them*.

Rather than seeing the Huxtables as a typical American family that happened to be black, I felt that many could not fathom that a black family had the kind of white family values represented on other shows; they were surprised, if not downright disbelieving, that a black family could be that "white."

This did not deter from the program's popularity or influence. It opened people's eyes to a new way of seeing a minority family. The characters were successful, articulate, educated and had strong family values. People of all races and ethnicities loved it. Along with "All in the Family" it is the only TV show to hold the top spot in the Nielsen ratings for five years.

I loved the show because it felt real. I knew families like the Huxtables, college-educated, professionally employed parents with children who attended college or legacy universities like Howard and Spelman. But I wonder how many people liked it because it felt like a fantasy, something along the lines of "well, we know this could never happen, but wouldn't it be nice if it did?"

Because when you consider that for decades the American media has mostly depicted poverty as a racial, mainly black, issue, how can anyone whose experience of black America is limited to what they see on TV think a successful black family could live in a nice neighborhood? They had never seen it before on their TV.

And they still don't.

Did you know there are twice as many white people living in poverty than black people? That's according to the U.S. Census Bureau's Historical Poverty Tables. 1959-2017. Yes, the percentage of blacks in poverty is higher than whites, 21 percent to 9 percent, but the difference in raw numbers based on overall population means that some 9.8 million blacks live in poverty while 17 million whites do.

However, according to *A Dangerous Distortion of Our Families,* found on colorofchange.org, a two-year study that analyzed national and local media in 2015 and 2016:

"Black families represent 59% of the poor in news and opinion media but make up just 27% of the poor... White families represent 17% of the poor in news and opinion media but make up 66% of the poor."

Let that sink in: There are twice as many whites living in poverty than blacks, but you are three times

MORE likely to see poor black folks in news and opinion stories. The same study found similar discrepancies in the portrayals of black and white families in terms of crime, welfare recipients and their stability.

No wonder so many people must have thought "The Cosby Show" was not an original sitcom reflecting some aspect of real life as much as it was an episode of "Fantasy Island" or "The Twilight Zone." Black people couldn't live this way!

For an even more contemporary example, a July 23, 2018 article on cnn.com showed that despite so much media reporting focusing in recent years on the terrible toll exacted on black men in this country, the share of black men in poverty has fallen from 41 percent in 1960 to 18 percent in 2018, and the percentage of black men in the middle or upper class, measured by family income, "has risen from 38 percent to 57 percent today. In other words, about one in two black men in America have reached the middle class or higher."

WHAT YOU TALKING 'BOUT WILLIS, INDEED!

Those numbers alone do not excuse racism on the personal or collective level, of course, and anyone who doesn't see that the scales of justice do not work in the favor of young men of color needs a wake-up call and a reminder of American history. Still, those numbers tell a much different story than that perpetuated by the media.

The fancy term for this is "racializing poverty," or reducing a very complicated issue with numerous factors into an easily grasped way: race. I call it pure and simple racism. Not the kind of overt racism found on a white supremacist website or, for that matter, Louis Farrakhan tweeting about the "Satanic Jew." It is a subtler, but pervasive, kind of racism that has come to be known as "institutional racism," or "systemic racism."

It is racism so ingrained in our social and political institutions that most of us accept it as the way things are done. Law enforcement profiling young men of color. Harsher sentences for crack cocaine (seen as a "black" drug) than cocaine (a more affluent and therefore "white" drug). Suspension rates among black and white students (three to one even though white students far outnumber black students).

Every one of those examples is also a stereotype: every young man of color in a hoodie is a thug; blacks only smoke cocaine; black students are just harder to discipline than whites. These stereotypes don't spring up overnight. They are distorted, clichéd images or an idea of someone or something in a particular group. Hear them enough, they become reinforced and lead to prejudices in the form of thinking associated with a specific group. That can lead to discrimination, which prompts negative actions toward anyone in that group.

And where do we get those stereotypes? Many times, from the people we know, our friends, our family members. But mostly from the stories we consume or, I should say, the stories fed to us. And who feeds us the most stories? The news and entertainment media.

If every news outlet is talking about something, such as the confirmation hearing of a prospective Supreme Court justice, then that's the story. There may be different spins, say *Fox News* versus *MSNBC* or the *Wall Street Journal* and the *New York Times*, but they're still talking about the same story and, over time, that creates a Grand Story, a narrative, almost like a story talking about itself.

The conventional narratives we have in this country, the stories we tell ourselves about ourselves and accept as definitive and accurate, all too often support the status quo. Even if they are false or inaccurate narratives that rely on stereotypes. These false narratives minimize complicated issues that should affect us all into someone else's problem. Isn't poverty an issue that should concern every American? Well, if the media is stereotyping black people as the ones who are poor, and I am not black, what does it matter to me? This also makes it easy to ignore or dismiss problems if our group isn't supposedly affected-- until they start happening to us. The opioid crisis wasn't front-page news when it was just black people in inner cities shooting up (as the narrative told us for years), but it sure was when white kids in the suburbs started popping pills (which did not happen overnight). There was no real government action on AIDS until this so-called "gay disease" started appearing in the straight community (that didn't happen overnight, either).

That is because the media is less interested in telling the American story, or narrative, than it is in reinforcing the parts that work for the status quo and dismissing or simplifying those that don't. Whether a conscious conspiracy or that the people who own the corporations that own the media outlets are overwhelmingly white men, as are most people who work for them, the reality is that whether producing news or entertainment, the media it deals heavily in stereotypes.

(I should also add that the influence of the American media isn't limited to solely Americans; it has created what I call a "global blueprint" for racism, an almost "Do It Yourself (DIY) effect," that creates a perpetual negative image of minorities, particularly black people, which sets the standard of bias in other countries,

For instance, my niece looks ethnically ambiguous. She identifies as black, but her skin color is light brown so she can pass just as easily as Spanish, Latina or Moroccan. But while studying abroad in Italy she noticed often when she told her Italian peers she was black, they started speaking to her in a stereotypically "urban voices," drawling out words like "Hevvy girl," and "sistah," and mocking how they thought black women acted, based on what they saw on American TV.

While the so-called hard news media of network and cable TV news programs projects its fair share of stereotypes, the entertainment media, the content producers of film and TV, is far more critical in supplying the stereotypes at the heart of institutionalized racism. Decades after "The Cosby Show" was the biggest hit on TV, the entertainment industry still traffics in marginalizing, negative stereotypes. Just as the use of the hyphen, or the idea behind it, marginalizes Americans into categories to render them less American, entertainment stereotypes do as well.

Throughout the 20th Century and into the 21st, Americans have consumed a constant diet of negative stereotypical characters based on race. Just off the top of my head, I can name:

*Speedy Gonzales,* the sleepy sombrero-clad cartoon character who could really move when he had to, but usually, like all Mexicans, would rather sleep all day.

*Little Black Sambo,* a racially insensitive depiction of a character from a children's book that used to line the walls of a family restaurant I remember as a child.

*Aunt Jemima,* the friendly, grossly overweight black mammy who lived to serve and had the syrup to prove it

*Huggy Bear,* the flamboyant, jive-talking hustler (and possibly pimp) who was a snitch to white cops on "Starsky and Hutch."

There are so many others, involving just about every group of people other than the dominant white American that benefits so much from not being broadly caricatured. From the "ancient Chinese secret" Calgon detergent ad in the 1970s (oh, those Chinese sure are a mysterious lot, aren't they?), to Tonto the "Indian," the stoic, always-faithful sidekick to the white Lone Ranger. Sure, it's "just entertainment," but my inescapable conclusion from a broad survey of depictions of people of color in the American media is that typecasting people of non-European descent as violent, lazy, and stupid encourages racial bigotry.

Even one of the most critically lauded shows of our time, HBO's "The Wire "depicted black men mainly as thugs, drug dealers and criminals. There are so many more, such as "Love and Hip Hop" a "reality" show that displays abusive and toxic relationships between black couples; Basketball Wives," which sexualizes black women and makes them trophy wives and reinforces the stereotype of the "angry black woman." You could say the same for "The Real Housewives of Atlanta."

We may no longer see signs directing non-whites to separate facilities; but we do see people of color portrayed as immoral such as the character of Cookie from the

HBO show "Empire," the wife of a former drug dealer turned hip-hop mogul, who gets released from prison and strikes out to lay claim to half of their multimillion-dollar record label, which was initially funded by her drug money. or characters on another HBO show, "Insecure." Or we see black characters fighting gang violence in the streets of LA, "Black Lightning," while the mostly white Marvel characters of "The Avengers" fight apocalyptic global enemies. What? A black character can't defend Earth because he or she is too busy defending the Hood?

Yes, these are fictional shows, but they are part of the same picture the mass media in America continues to propagate: that the only environment black people could ever know is one of crime, poverty, abuse and toxicity--or they are drawn from the other extreme, more peaceful, but still a terrible distortion: the docile servant, such as every black character in the critically acclaimed show "Mad Men." This reinforces the domestic stereotype. And that stereotype has a long history.

One of the most controversial figures in entertainment history was Lincoln Theodore Monroe Perry, better known as Stepin Fetchit, his trademark character. You might think his status as the first black actor with a successful career in Hollywood was progress. But consider Fetchit's billing: "The Laziest Man in America." Not only was this portrayal of blacks incredibly insulting and degrading, but Perry's role as Fetchit –

displayed in 44 films between 1927 and 1939, shown across America-- was probably the most seen portrayal of a black person in history up to that time. Who knows how many people made the blanket assumption that the only black character they saw on screen was accurate? He was harmless and servile and served as a prototype for one of the Hollywood fantasies of black men for so long: a good darkie who knew how to stay in his correct place.

Ironically, depicting blacks as unintelligent, worthless, childlike individuals who needed instructions for the simplest tasks, skyrocketed Fetchit (and Perry) to fame and fortune. While there's no denying he was talented and a pioneer in his field, it also left many Americans with a biased view of black people as mumbling, shiftless vagabonds unable to contribute in any meaningful way to society. His fame came at the price of reinforcing, if not downright helping to create, horrific stereotypes.

Then there is the angry black woman stereotype, which has its roots in 19th Century America minstrel shows in which, as Ritu Prasad wrote on bbb.com on September 2018, "black women were often played by overweight white men who painted their faces black and donned fat suits to "make them look less than human, unfeminine, ugly. Their main way of interacting with the men around them was to scream and fight and come off angry, irrationally so, in response to the circumstances around them."

Is Tyler Perry doing anything different in his "Madea" franchise, which offers the sexually non-threatening, overweight unattractive black woman who mother-hens everyone? While wildly successful, that portrayal uses the angry black woman trope, a fixed image in many people's minds that, if translated into the real world, renders any outspoken black woman as ill-mannered and sassy (Maxine Waters, anyone?)

But volumes can be written about media portrayals of black women, from Jamie Foxx's character of Wanda Wayne from "In Living Color" to Martin Lawrence's Sheneneh in "Martin." Using black women as comic relief, often when they are angry, only minimizes the validity of real-life black women's thoughts and actions.

Perry, Foxx and Lawrence are all talented, wealthy and successful black men. So the fact they peddle in the same stereotypes as the mostly white men who are atop the media industry must be part of this discussion, as does self-empowerment and personal responsibility.

Due to their celebrity, entertainers in the public eye need to remember their choices affect far more people than most people's. Like it or not, they are role models, and while they have a right to their personal lives and not to have every one of their decisions magnified and exaggerated, I feel through their work they should undoubtedly strive for more responsibility. However, there are still minority entertainers of various ethnicities who keep the negative stereotypes alive by perpetuating them.

Maybe they believe if the media insists on portraying their ethnic group negatively that someone with an authentic perspective should be the one using the stereotype. That would make them "in on the joke." However, all too often, these portrayals, even in films or TV shows targeted at minority audiences, are reminiscent of the humiliating and demeaning roles Stepin Fetchit pioneered. This is evident in some recent comedies and dramas, like "Nothing to Lose," "Soul Plane," "Madea's Family Reunion," and "Precious." It is time to stop passing off negative stereotypes as comedy or "art" and start accurately depicting all ethnic cultures respectfully.

As a beautiful example of how self-empowerment and personal responsibility can bridge the stereotype gap, consider Halle Berry. The first significant character she played in a film, "Jungle Fever" was a ghetto girl, AKA a hood rat. However, she was strong enough to believe in her talent and chose her future roles wisely, and now she ranks among the most well-respected actresses in Hollywood. It's just a shame she is an exception—albeit an exceptional one—rather than so typical we forget to notice her race.

However, I'm pleased to see a very surprising, stirring awakening has begun to bloom. That renaissance includes the 2017 Jordan Peele film "Get Out" It was groundbreaking in using a black lead character in a suspenseful horror film. Although it dealt with racism, it handled it without stereotypical biases. It was subtler in illustrating the ignorance and assumptions of many people that influence their perceptions when based solely on the color of another person's skin. For instance, many of the white characters in "Get Out," viewed a black man as someone who had to be athletic, endowed with generous physical attributes and genetically slower to age. They did not see this person as a whole, intelligent human, but as a vessel for a caricature to inhabit.

Another positive step was Ryan Coogler's 2018 "Black Panther. I usually do not attend movies regularly (I wait until it comes to Netflix). However, I made an exception for this because of all the calls I received from friends and family telling me I *must* see it. I was not disappointed. It was an incredible cinematic triumph, and not just because it grossed $1.3 billion. It was its amazingly powerful and positive representation of people of color.

Then there's another Peele film, 2019's "Us." It shattered all expectations about how race was " supposed" to be dealt with in a movie by not discussing it at all. It forced viewers to ask themselves, as Peele said, "Why did I think a movie with black people had to be about blackness?" The positive reaction "Us" received from the media only proves stereotypes aren't needed to make a successful film.

Yes, these are all positive developments, and I can't wait for the day when the buzz around Oscar nominees is over artistic vision and skill rather than race. But there is a long way to go before Hollywood's present catches up to its past. Consider that since the first Academy Awards in 1929, only 17 black actors or actresses have ever received an Oscar in any the four acting categories, less than half of one percent (17 out of 356 Oscars). But then you look at the type of characters these performers portrayed, and you start to scratch your head: two slaves, a prostitute, a swindler, a psychotic cop, a depraved abusive mother, a maid.

The numbers are even starker for America's two other largest groups of minorities: five Latinos have earned Oscars in the four categories, and four Asians.

Again: Hollywood seems to be making a more concerted push to be more inclusive of minorities—and examples like Peele and the "Black Panther" film are proof, but it also seems self-evident that much of the entertainment industry is content with still casting things in the ethnic stereotype box. Recent examples include "All American," about a black teen from Crenshaw who transfers to a high school in Beverly Hills and everyone judges him because he's from the "ghetto." Or the movie "The Hate You Give," about a black girl who lives in a poverty-stricken, crime-riddled mostly black neighborhood who attends a wealthy white prep school.

Or "Devious Maids," about women of Latin descent who work for wealthy white people in Beverly Hills, juggling being maids with all the (ethnic) drama that comes with it. Or the TV sitcom "Fresh off the Boat," about the life of an Asian immigrant family in America that is like an Asian version of "Good Times," not in terms of their income, but the vast Asian stereotypes.

The continued use of these stereotypes is a gross insult to the history of this country. Through America's 245-year history, people of color have made significant strides towards independence and equality. Despite the constitutional rights and influence that people of color have gained, the bigoted dogmas and preconceived ideas programmed into the American psyche have changed very little. The negative stereotypes used to form the mental attitude of American citizens for so long have reorganized into more subtle and insidious types of racism. Today's racism is a more polished and sophisticated brand of discrimination, and it is the crowning achievement of the American mass media.

I believe the best way to defeat this type of ignorance is to withhold what its producers most want: your hard-earned cash. Boycotting a movie makes a statement because it hits producers where it hurts most. Only by this direct message can we hope to exile these stereotypical portrayals rather than continue enabling them.

It is time to say, "No. No, I will not go to the movies and watch your racist rhetoric. No, I will not buy your brand. No, I will not view your television series if you don't portray me fairly and respectfully."

I have heard various reasons why the media remains locked into stereotyping, usually concerning the restricted amount of airtime, cost, and that stereotyping is "easy and convenient" because portrayed individuals don't need a personality.

Now, this might be acceptable if those stereotypes weren't negative; but all too often they are. The black guy playing basketball (Dr. Pepper commercial). The black woman with the down-home lingo selling cleaning supplies or chicken (Pine-Sol and Popeye's Chicken). The short Mexican wrestler (Burger King commercial). In a print ad, Nivea showed a clean-cut, well-dressed black man toss the head of a black man with stubble and an afro, with the caption, "Re-Civilize Yourself."

I can't count how many times I have been stereotyped. When I was younger, I wanted to be an actor and even found an agent who sent me on many auditions. It was so disheartening that most roles I auditioned were streetwalkers, gangsters, drug addicts, and other "black life" stereotypes. A further indignity: the most common comment from casting was they liked how I played the role, but that I didn't sound "black enough" or "street enough." I innocently believed that since I was black, I didn't need to be told how to sound black.

Stereotyping also surfaces in my personal life, and the assumption that my skin color makes me an expert on how to speak "real" black ( do Barack Obama and Chris Rock talk the same?) isn't the only broad generalization.

Consider these questions I have often been asked:

*Why do people of color...* ...Really? Newsflash: I am not the national spokesperson for every person of color in America.

*"Can I feel your hair?"* followed by a surprised comment at its softness, not the steel wool they expected to feel.

*You sound like you're white.* Not a stereotype per se, but it ticks me off, as it implies only Caucasian people possess the intellectual capacity to be articulate.

Then there's the running joke among my female friends, regardless of ethnicity, of the traits I must possess, based on advertisements and commercials featuring or targeted to black women.

I only listen to hip-hop or gospel.

I am overweight

I'm in a non-speaking role

I'm your target if you are aiming your fast food product at an "urban" audience

If I am in a commercial with children, I am shown as a single mother instead of as a member of a nuclear family.

But while laughing at the ridiculousness of stereotypes is a healthy option, that shouldn't preclude us from realizing the devastating effects stereotypes can produce. Particularly for children. According to a 1998 article in *Reality in Television,* quoting Ray Wayne:

*"Considerable public concern has arisen over the issue of media diversity, as it is generally accepted that mass media has strong social and psychological effects on viewers.*

*Film and television, for example, provide many children with their first exposure to people of other races, ethnicities, religions, and cultures. What they see onscreen, therefore, can impact their attitudes about the treatment of others.*

*One study found, for instance, that two years of viewing Sesame Street by European-American preschoolers was associated with more positive attitudes toward African and Latino Americans. Another study found that white children exposed to a negative television portrayal of African-Americans had an adverse change in attitude toward blacks."*

That article reveals how vulnerable children are to messages propagated by the media. It is incumbent upon all Americans to demand accurate portrayals of everyone without preconception or bias. We are all responsible for ensuring negative imagery does not bombard children.

Now, I know some readers are thinking, "but I'm not a kid, Nicole. I am a rational, critical thinking, intelligent person, and my perception is not skewed regardless of how many stereotypes I see in the media." Maybe that's true on an individual level, but collectively I don't think there's any question the media wields enormous influence on people's reality.

It is what a significant mass media theorist, Walter Lippman addressed in his influential 1922 book "Public Opinion," in which he examined the role the mass media plays in stereotypes. He believed that the world was "too big, too complex and too fleeting for direct acquaintance between people and their environment." So we build a " pseudo-environment that is a subjective, biased, and necessarily abridged mental image of the world, and to a degree, everyone's pseudo-environment is a fiction."

That pseudo-environment, Lippman argued, is made up of pictures in our mind. However, because the world is too complicated, those pictures are shaped in large part by that which has been "explored, reported, and imagined by others." Each of us subjectively processes those pictures, and over time, those pictures become more real than what we are seeing.

If Lippman was right, if the pictures in our mind, our subjective reality, is more "real" than objective reality, and if the mass media is responsible for generating most of those pictures, then it stands to reason that whoever controls those pictures, that information, has an unbelievable amount of power.

And who owns the media and thus control over what information is disseminated? A widely circulated graphic, "The Illusion of Choice," which surfaced in 2012, showed that 90 percent of what we read, watched and listened to was produced and distributed by six mega-corporations that owned most of our news and entertainment channels, stations, studios, newspapers, etc. The percentages and lineups have changed since then (for instance: Disney now also owns the Star War franchise) and the entry of internet-based companies into original programming, such as Amazon and Netflix, is impacting it, but the reality is that corporate profits, not accurate representations of reality, drives most of our media.

What that means, according to friends of mine who work in the industry, is that sponsors, or advertisers, do not want to alienate viewers associating themselves with programming, or running advertisements, that might offend the highest number of people, And the last time I checked the U.S. numbers, in 2017, almost 77 percent of American considered themselves white.

Until there is more minority representation in terms of who owns and works for the media, the pictures of America that many of us have in our heads will not change. For even though the face of the nation is changing demographically, the media remains the same. The producers, investors, and media bigwigs are woefully out of touch. Moreover, their disconnect filters into the perspectives of many of their consumers.

In the U.K., there has been a strong push to eradicate this divisive mindset by using diverse and inclusive images, not just of all ethnicities, but people from all historically marginalized backgrounds. One image that resonated with me was a permanently disfigured news commentator who had been severely burned in an accident. Upon his recovery, he went back to his job as a commentator.

I seldom see that kind of bravery, forward-thinking, and inclusiveness on American television. Here, an idealized normal is what we see on our news programs, with the majority of American newscasters and TV hosts sounding exactly alike, with interchangeable cookie-cutter appearances.

Yes, it's all about ratings and the assumption is that viewers will watch a pretty person on TV longer than someone who doesn't embody the conventional definition of pretty. But, again, those images, continuously broadcast and absorbed, can create a picture in someone's mind of what is real. In this case, it's that the only people qualified to deliver the news of the day in America are well dressed, well-spoken, attractive white people.

I believe the industry fully understands its power and uses it to shape what it thinks the public should believe. Is it not about time Americans speak for themselves and stop allowing the media to dupe us into a false reality that supports the status quo?

The American people aren't sheep. But even though there seems to be a widespread lack of trust in the media, as in all our institutions these days, which our current president has plugged into with his attack on the media as "fake" or "an enemy of the people," I believe most Americans still blindly accept the baseless assumptions of American media. Yes, the public needs to engage in more critical thinking, but I feel that media portrayals of minorities are so normalized that many people don't begin to think for themselves, let alone question anything.

The racial stereotypes that the media reinforces dovetails with my objection to the use of ethnicity (through the hyphen and the concept it represents) to define many Americans. Both use race to limit, or to take away from the natural birthright of anyone born here, or the right obtained by becoming a citizen: being an American. Both strip individuality from a person, either by associating them with negative, inaccurate caricatures or lumping them in with a group of people they may have very little in common with. Both use race and ethnicity as the primary definition of an American. All too often, for those unable or ill-equipped to stand up for their individuality, their Americanism, that definition shapes the course their life takes.

One of my professors at Yale, Dr. Paul Bloom, made a point I felt was very compelling regarding this mindset:

*The problem is that there's a lot of evidence that even when we don't want to rely on stereotypes, even when we consciously believe that we are not biased, nonetheless we are influenced by them and fall back upon them. In an interesting way, we are at war with ourselves."*

What difference does all this make in the real world, and why should we pay any attention to these implicit biases?

Perception shapes our actions. These TV shows and movies may be fictitious, but the results that stem from stereotypes are real. Prejudice is real; discrimination is real. Ignoring it only furthers a discriminatory and divisive illusion. Let us not forget the so-called "foundations" of our American values of equality and acceptance. American reality is not what we see on our screens but what we see in our homes, our neighborhoods, our communities.

In that respect, Hollywood and the rest of the media's reliance on stereotypes and fostering a sense of racial disharmony is a losing battle. America is diversifying at an exponential rate. As a case study, I bring up something that I have already established is very close to my heart: interracial relationships.

Even though six years old, I doubt the data from a Pew Research Center 2013 census regarding the rise of intermarriage is any lower in 2019.

"Marriage across racial and ethnic lines continues to be on the rise in the United States. The share of new marriages between spouses of different races or ethnicities increased to 15.1% in 2010, and the share of all current marriages that are either interracial or interethnic has reached an all-time high of 8.4%. The upward trend of intermarriage is many decades old."

This is my reality; this is what I see at my family gatherings. My brother's wife was Korean/black; one of my sisters has a Japanese boyfriend; my other sister's husband is German/Ecuadorian, and my ex-sister-in-law is Guamanian. All the children from these various unions are beautiful and represent the changing face of American people in general. I want to see that portrayed as the portrait of an American family.

However, while America is blending into a more diverse mosaic, all my siblings have experienced the subtleties of racism because of whom they chose to love. Sometimes this happens intentionally because of personal prejudice, and sometimes unintentionally. For even though there are more interracial couples than ever, the fact they are so rarely depicted honestly in the media means many Americans still view is as odd, or different.

Millions of Americans are in interracial relationships, but millions more still are not used to seeing people of different ethnicities romantically depicted in the media. But interracial relationships are real. This is our new normal. Moreover, I am convinced that although it will take time, ultimately, love truly will conquer all.

# CHAPTER NINE

---

# HOW CAN WE CHANGE?

*"Being able to live without having to be defined by your
skin color is the hallmark of privilege."*

—Luvvie Ajayi

Many people believe there is too much focus on race in this country. That if we would just stop talking about race and making it a constant issue, all the problems associated with it would disappear.

I'm betting most of those people are also white and have enjoyed the luxury of living their entire lives as full citizens of this country, not saddled with a label and confined to an ethnic box that makes them feel they're a little bit American, but not completely.

Others believe that the story of race *is* the story of America, encompassing the essential questions of

America: What is freedom? What is justice? What is equality? What is America?

I want to think those are the people who genuinely care about America. For they realize the past informs the present, and it is only through that recognition can we make our future brighter by inspiring change, enlivening our mind and spirit, thinking and growing, and challenging the status quo.

Part of all that is realizing that no one has the right to define you as a person, or human being, based on your skin color. And then standing up and voicing your opinion. Do not allow yourself to be hyphenated. Do not stay in a box by checking the box.

But along with that realization comes another: we must work diligently not to define *ourselves* by our skin color. For just as when we allow others to determine who and what we are based on race it becomes a crutch, the same can be said for when we make our skin color the focal point of our identity. Each is a trap to be avoided.

I know how easily that trap ensnares people. It happens after being bombarded with negative image after negative image of who or what we are supposed to be. Given enough time and with no one in our circle of influence providing positive feedback, that can lead us to accept our status as second-class citizens. That is a reality that many people of color face in America. I understand that and feel deeply for them, I genuinely do. But I also know that for some, victimization can be seductive. It means "it isn't my fault! Someone or something else is doing this to me."

For example, I have spoken to young people of color many times, and some claim they cannot succeed because the odds are against them. But when I ask what they have done to succeed, I find many have never tried. They believe they are victims, so what's the point in trying? But while it is important to protect one's self, where is the line between self-protective and closed-off? When "Because I am black" or another race becomes an explanation for every setback, it can lead to emotional exhaustion, and people stop trying to achieve. We must urge young people to realize that they need to own their actions even when the odds are seemingly against them.

To quote Martin Luther King Jr. in "Three Ways of Meeting Oppression:"

*"There is such a thing as the freedom of exhaustion. Some people are so worn down by the yoke of oppression that they give up. But this is not the way out. To accept passively an unjust system is to cooperate with that system; thereby the oppressed become as evil as the oppressor. Noncooperation with evil is as much a moral obligation as is cooperation with good. The oppressed can never allow the conscience of the oppressor to slumber."*

I have been blessed to know many people of color who overcame negative situations and tremendous odds, but overcame the crutch mindset and achieved great success. While their stories have all been different, I'd bet every one of them could look back at the course of their life and find one person who believed in them or pushed them to achieve. It may have been a teacher, minister, family member, or coach who taught them that self-respect, personal responsibility, and personal pride are the keys to success. We should all endeavor to incorporate those things more into our lives, to strive to be better, to inspire young people to do the same.

But coming from a position where race is the most essential thing about others, or where race and ethnicity is the most important thing about ourselves, is not the way to inspire change. There is no room in today's America to be proud merely because your skin is of a particular hue; the content of your character is what you should be proud of. Pride in one's skin color is one of the most divisive concepts in American history; this applies to all ethnicities. You should be proud of the person you are inside your skin, rather than the color of it.

I would be less than honest if I did not admit that people of color, in some part, contribute to the racial divide. Anti-black resentment in the Latinx community and vice versa. The unfortunate favoring of lighter skin over darker skin within so many communities. The "day of absence," in 2017 at a Washington state university when white people were basically kicked off campus. All those hinder, not help, racial reconciliation.

And, I think, so does one tradition in the black community that few people object to: Black History Month. When it commenced, it was needed. Now, the point has been made. I know many people are going to be shocked, dismayed, or angry at that statement, but I do have a logical reason. I believe black history should be part of the regular curriculum in American history and not something you have to go out of your way to study separately. Real American history could never be told without including black Americans. Black people have been in America and created history in America from its Colonial beginnings. It is inarguable that black history is American history, and conversely, American history is black history. To teach black history in a vacuum lessens its actual impact and value to American history as a whole. By the way, that vacuum happens to be February, the shortest month of the year!

Now, I do not mean that Americans who happen to be black should shy away from their history. For example, I often hear some version of this: "If Jewish people can forgive Germans for the Holocaust, why can't black people forgive white people for slavery?" And many white people may ask the question, "Why should I feel guilty for a crime that I didn't commit, but my ancestors did?"

Let's look at it this way: Germans have reckoned with their past. They deliberately speak about the Nazi regime and the atrocities that were committed as early as elementary school. In contrast, there are a significant number of white Americans TODAY who support Confederate monuments in public spaces, monuments built in large part to honor resistance to black civil rights. The legislation that crowned the Civil Rights era passed less than 60 years ago.

It's illegal to be a Nazi in Germany. But Americans still debate whether or not the Confederate flag is a legitimate symbol of American ideals.

With these shortcomings of American conduct, we also need to take a hard look at the labels we've accepted, such as African American. As previously mentioned, the label was picked up by Jesse Jackson, which caused the media to embrace it and, eventually, most black people in America. This was the terminology used by one political figure, and it has been forced down the throats of black people for the last 30 years. This is something we as Americans of all ethnicities could change. Do not allow yourself to be hyphenated. Do not check the box; do not answer to any description but American.

I believe America one day will be a country where Americans view one another as fellow Americans. It will not come without difficulty, however. A mass awakening is needed. Too many Americans are unaware of the problem, or are too comfortable or settled, or don't know how to turn their private frustration into public action. And it would be naïve for anyone to think advocating on behalf of those who draw the short straw in our democracy can be done without friction.

Consider two of the most significant broad movements in our country's history, one based around ethnicity, the other gender: The Civil Rights Movement, and the Women's Rights Movement. Though each struggled against great resistance, both persevered largely because they triggered a great awakening among many Americans. But neither happened because people stayed immobile, or pointed fingers, or felt trapped by their second-class status. They organized, strategized, and worked tirelessly toward social justice and giving marginalized people a voice, which created substantial change.

None of the successes those movements achieved, and are still trying to achieve, from gender equity to housing discrimination, would have been possible without acknowledging our differences, and the structural inequities in our society that work against many of us perceived as being different. But there are some Americans who don't want to admit that. And why should they? One of the unique comforts of privilege is that it evinces a degree of removal from the everyday experience of being a minority in this country. From that perch, it is easy to say that things will get better, and we're all the same.

But I tend to think there is a sense of underlying among those who live with that privilege, maybe something deep inside that comprehends they are the fortunate ones by only an accident of birth. And they're terrified it's going to be stripped from them. Why else do so many white Americans, when they think of immigration, turn aggressive over feeling anxious about "losing our country." Or bristle when hearing "black lives matter," or love to say others are playing the race card or can't stand hearing about slavery since "It was so long ago and can't they just get over it?"

Maybe it boils down to this: just as ethnic minorities may feel alienated from white America due to their labels and other factors discussed in this book, white Americans feel alienated from a more racially diverse American that they may, consciously or not, don't view as the real America when in reality it's as real as American gets. It's that America on the other side of the racial and class (and, one could easily argue, gender and sexual orientation) divides. They don't understand it, so they don't want to hear about it.

But willing ignorance won't change reality. Nor is thinking that talking about how minorities' experiences differ and working to address inequality, instead of concentrating on how we're the same, is inherently "un-American."

I certainly don't believe that. I am arguing that embracing and encouraging minorities' voices is not only good politics but also a necessary component of a healthy democracy; and that one of the great strengths of America is our differences. People are people, and everything about them contributes to making them unique: from their belief systems and political leanings to their personal experiences and, yes, their race. But those differences should not separate us and make us weak and fractured as a country, reducing us to bickering tribes and leading to nativism or outright racism. Our differences are what make us stronger when we come together, for we each bring something of our own to the metaphorical table, and to the project that I am calling "Don't Check the Box," just one step on an even larger project that began on July 1, 1776 (the date the Declaration of Independence was really signed): the Ongoing Building of America.

Some readers may think I am contradicting myself, playing both sides. On the one hand, I say abolish the hyphen and the labels that put people of color into boxes that keep them separate and viewed as less than fully American; on the other, I am saying that we need to recognize that racial differences are important.

I don't think that is a wishy-washy opinion. Because for this grand experiment called American Democracy to continue, we don't have to overcome or abolish race, we need to change the mindset of race. We need to change the concept from "there are ethnic minorities who happen to be American," to "there are Americans who happen to be ethnic minorities," and their experiences, work, and dreams are as crucial to the shaping of the future of this country as anyone else's. By changing that mindset, by changing the very words we use, we can come closer to finally making good on the promise of equality that (some of) the words embedded in our founding documents tell us what America was intended to be.

And that means examining how our society has and is currently falling short and working to address them. And I say let's start with getting rid of all labels, hyphenated or not, and acknowledging that we are all, first and foremost, equal citizens of the same country and we're all heading in the same direction, so why not work with, rather than against, each other to get there?

**So, I ask you, my fellow Americans, don't you think now is the time to dismantle our mantles, to stop checking boxes, and to start rocking the boat?**

# WHAT IS HYPHENED-NATION?

*Hyphened-Nation was inspired by my travels overseas, and time spent living in the United Kingdom. Living abroad was an eye-opening experience, I grew to understand certain aspects of American culture better, the longer I lived overseas. This book is about my insights and experience of being treated as a pure American, not a hyphenated one. The difference was startling, and lead me on a journey to understand why The United States is one of the only, if not the only country, that hyphenates its citizens by ethnicity before nationality.*

*Those same boxes we allow ourselves to be placed into as hyphenated-Americans, limit our economic, educational, societal and cultural growth. This book focuses on ways the U.S. and Europe differ culturally via media, and how a bridge might be created. I hope this book inspires you to join the movement and, "Don't Check the Box." Be a catalyst for positive change.*

*Your stories and insights will help to light everyone's path to a brighter future.*

Connect with Us!

Instagram Facebook Twitter

# BIBLIOGRAPHY

The Constitution of the United States. The Bill of Rights & All Amendments

Bronfenbrenner, M. (1982). "Hyphenated Americans. Economic Aspects."

[*Law and Contemporary Problems*, 55(2), 9.

Coates, Ta-Nehisi (2013, May, 13). "What We Mean When We Say Race Is a Social Construct." *The Atlantic.*

Du Bois W. E. B., and Henry Louis Gates. (2016.) *Black Reconstruction in America: the Oxford W.E.B Du Bois.* Oxford University Press.

Gannon, M. (2016, Feb). "Race Is a Social Construct, Scientists Argue." *Scientific American.*

Gerstle, G. (2017). *American Crucible: Race and Nation in the Twentieth Century.* Princeton University Press.

Gosling, M. (1999, June) 3. "The Role of Television with Regard to Racial Stereotypes. *Poverty & Prejudice Media and Race.*

Greenwald, A. G. & Banaji, M. R. (1995). "Implicit social cognition: Attitudes, self-esteem, and stereotypes." *Psychological Review,* 102, 4-27.

Horton, Y., Price, R., Brown, E. (1999, June 1). "Portrayal of Minorities in the Film, Media and Entertainment Industries." *Journals on Poverty & Prejudice: Media and Race.*

"Intermarriage on the Rise in the U.S." (2013, Jan). *Pew Research Center,,* www.pewresearch.org/.

Jacobson, M. (2003). *Whiteness of a Different Color: European Immigrants and the Alchemy of Race.* Harvard University Press.

Lencker, J N, editor. (1916, April). "Insulting Slogans Divide a United Nation." *Northern Review,* 2 (3), 21-24.

Mediascope. (1998). *Picture This: Diversity In Film And Television."* Prentice-Hall, New Jersey, NH.

Muske-Dukes, C., (2002, Dec. 29). "A Lost Eloquence." *New York Times.*

Ochberg, F., (2005, April 8).
"The Ties That Bind Captive to Captor." *Los Angeles Times,*

Roediger, D., (2007). *The Wages Of Whiteness.* London: Verso.

Salerno, A. E. (1996). "America for Americans Only: Gino C. Speranza and the Immigrant Experience." *Italian Americana* 14(2) 133-47.

"Roosevelt Bars the Hyphyenate" (1915. Oct. 13 ). *New York Times*

Spickard, P. 2007. *Almost All Aliens: Race, Colonialism, and Immigration in American History and Identity.* Routledge, 2007.

Spickard, P. 2007. "Whither the Asian American Coalition?" *Pacific Historical Review,* 76(4), 585-604.

Vedantam, S. (2005, Jan.. 23). "See No Bias." *Washington Post*

Wawro, Geoffrey. (2018, Sept. 12). "How 'Hyphenated Americans' Won World War I." *New York Times*

Wilkerson, I., (2010). *The Warmth Of Other Suns.* New York: Vintage Books.

Williamson, C. (1997). *The Immigration Mystique: America's False Conscience*. AICF, 1997.

Zolberg,   A. R. 2008. *A Nation By Design*. Harvard University Pres.

Made in the USA
Coppell, TX
03 July 2020